Nick Vandome

iPad
for Seniors

in
easy steps

7th edition
covers all versions of iPad with iOS 11

In easy steps is an imprint of In Easy Steps Limited
16 Hamilton Terrace · Holly Walk · Leamington Spa
Warwickshire · United Kingdom · CV32 4LY
www.ineasysteps.com

Seventh Edition

In Easy Steps Limited supports The Forest Stewardship Council (FSC),
the leading international forest certification organization. All our titles
that are printed on Greenpeace approved FSC certified paper carry the
FSC logo.

MIX
Paper from
responsible sources
FSC   FSC® C020837
www.fsc.org

Printed and bound in the United Kingdom

ISBN 978-1-84078-790-0

Contents

11 Traveling Companion 165

12 Practical Matters 179

Index 187

1 Choosing your iPad

It's compact, it's stylish, it's powerful; and it's perfect for anyone, of any age. This chapter introduces the iPad, the iOS 11 operating system and some of the basic controls and buttons, so you can quickly get up and running with this exciting tablet.

The iEverything

The iPad is a tablet computer that has gone a long way to change how we think of computers and how we interact with them. Instead of a large, static object it is effortlessly mobile, and even makes a laptop seem bulky by comparison.

But even with its compact size, the iPad still manages to pack a lot of power and functionality into its diminutive body. In this case small is most definitely beautiful, and the range of what you can do with the iPad is considerable:

- Communicate via email, video and text messaging.

- Surf the web wirelessly.

- Add an endless number of new "apps" from the Apple App Store.

- Use a range of entertainment tools, covering music, photos, video, books and games.

- Do all of your favorite productivity tasks such as word processing, creating spreadsheets or producing presentations.

- Organize your life with apps for calendars, address books, notes, reminders, and much more.

"Apps" is just a fancy name for what are more traditionally called programs in the world of computing. The iPad has several apps that come built in and ready for use. There are thousands more available to download from the online App Store (see Chapter 5, pages 86-91).

The New icon pictured above indicates a new or enhanced feature introduced with iPads using iOS 11.

Add to this up to 10 hours' battery life when you are on the move, a range of different sizes (with a Retina Display screen of outstanding clarity) and a seamless backup system, and it is clear why the iPad can stylishly fulfill all of your computing needs.

Simplicity of the iPad

Computers have become a central part of our everyday lives, but there is no reason why they need to be complex devices that have us scratching our heads as to how to best use them. The iPad is not only stylish and compact; it also makes the computing process as simple as possible, so you can concentrate on what you want to do. Some ways in which this is done are:

- **Instantly on**. With the iPad there is no long wait for it to turn on, or wake from a state of sleep. When you turn it on, it is ready to use; it's as simple as that.

- **Apps**. iPad apps sit on the Home screen, visible and ready to use. Most apps are created in a similar format, so once you have mastered getting around them you will be comfortable using most apps.

- **Settings**. One of the built-in iPad apps is Settings. This is a one-stop shop for customizing the way that your iPad looks and operates, and also how settings for apps work.

The Dock is the bar at the bottom of the iPad screen, onto which apps can be placed for quick access.

- **Dock and App Switcher Window**. These are two functions that enable you to access your favorite apps quickly, regardless of what you are doing on your iPad.

- **Home button**. This enables you to return to the main Home screen at any time. It also has some additional functionality, depending on how many times you click it.

Models and Sizes

Since its introduction in 2010, the iPad has evolved in both its size and specifications. It is now a family of devices, rather than a single size. When choosing your iPad, the first consideration is which size to select. There are three options:

- **iPad**. This is the original version of the iPad, and retains the standard iPad title (although some previous versions were called iPad Air). It measures 9.7 inches (diagonal) and has a high-resolution Retina Display screen. At the time of printing, the latest version is the seventh generation of the standard-size iPads.

- **iPad Mini**. The iPad Mini is similar in most respects to the larger version, including the Retina Display screen, except for its size. The screen is 7.9 inches (diagonal) and it is also slightly lighter. The latest version (at the time of printing) is the iPad Mini 4.

- **iPad Pro**. This is the latest version of the iPad to be introduced, and is a very powerful all-round iPad. It comes with either a 10.5- or a 12.9-inch screen. The iPad Pro can also be used with the Apple Pencil stylus and the detachable Apple Smart Keyboard (both bought separately). The Smart Keyboard (see page 13 for more details) has a Smart Connector to attach it to the iPad Pro, and this ensures it works as soon as it is attached. The Apple Pencil (see page 12 for more details) has to be "paired" with the iPad Pro, which involves opening **Settings** > **Bluetooth** and turning Bluetooth **On**.

Then, attach the Apple Pencil to the iPad Pro via the Lightning Connector. It should then be paired and ready for use. The Apple Pencil can be used for selecting items on screen (by tapping), swiping pages, and drawing and writing with appropriate apps.

Don't forget

Another variation in the iPad family is how they connect to the internet and online services. This is either with just Wi-Fi connectivity or Wi-Fi and 4G connectivity (where available, but it also covers 3G). This should be considered if you will need to connect to the internet with a cellular connection when you are traveling away from home. 4G and 3G enable you to connect to a mobile network to access the internet, in the same way as with a cell/mobile phone. This requires a contract with a provider of this type of service.

Hot tip

The iPad Pro is an excellent option, particularly for typing with the Smart Keyboard.

Specifications Explained

Most models of iPad have the same range of specifications (the main difference being the screen sizes). Some of the specifications to consider are:

- **Processor**: This determines the speed at which the iPad operates and how quickly tasks are performed.

- **Storage**: This determines how much content you can store on your iPad. Across the iPad family, the range of storage is 32GB, 64GB, 128GB, 256GB or 512GB.

- **Connectivity**: The options for this are Wi-Fi and 3G/4G connectivity for the internet, and Bluetooth for connecting to other devices over short distances.

- **Cameras**: The front-facing camera is a FaceTime one, which is best for video calls or "selfies" (self-portraits). The back-facing camera is a high-resolution iSight one that takes excellent photos and videos.

- **Screen**: iPads that can run iOS 11 all have Retina Display screens for the highest resolution and best clarity. This is an LED-backlit screen.

- **Operating system**: The latest version of the iPad operating system is iOS 11.

- **Battery power**: This is the length of time the iPad can be used for general use, such as surfing the web on Wi-Fi, watching video, or listening to music. All models offer approximately 10 hours of use in this way.

- **Input/Output**: These include a Lightning connector port (for charging), 3.5 mm stereo headphone minijack, built-in speaker, microphone and nano-SIM card tray (Wi-Fi and 4G model only).

- **Sensors**: These are used to determine the amount of ambient light and also the orientation in which the iPad is being held. The sensors include an accelerometer, ambient light sensor, barometer and gyroscope.

The amount of storage you need may change once you have bought your iPad. If possible, buy a version with as much as possible, as you cannot add more later.

The iSight camera on the iPad and the iPad Mini 4 is 8 megapixels; on the iPad Pro 10.5 and 12.9 inch it is 12 megapixels.

You can connect your iPad to a High-Definition TV (HDTV), with AirPlay Mirroring. To do this you will need an Apple Lightning Digital AV Adapter or an Apple Lightning to VGA Adapter (sold separately).

Apple Pencil

The Apple Pencil is a stylus that can be used on the screen instead of your finger to perform a variety of tasks. At the time of printing, it is only compatible with the iPad Pro models and can be used for some of the following:

The Apple Pencil can be used to annotate PDF documents or screenshots on the iPad Pro, simply by writing on them. This is known as Instant Markup, and is a new feature in iOS 11.

- Drawing intricate (or simple) artwork using drawing or painting apps.

- Moving around web pages by swiping or tapping on links to access other web pages.

- Selecting items of text by tapping on them and also dragging the selection handles.

- Annotating PDF documents.

Charging the Apple Pencil

To annotate a screenshot, press and hold the On/Off button and Home button simultaneously to capture the screenshot. A thumbnail of the screenshot appears in the bottom left-hand corner for a few seconds. Tap once on this to expand it, and use the drawing tools at the bottom of the screen to annotate it. The annotated image can then be saved into the Photos app.

The Apple Pencil can be charged using the iPad Lightning connector port (the same one as for charging the iPad) or the iPad's charging cable, using the Apple Pencil's Lightning connector adapter, which is supplied with the Apple Pencil.

To check the level of Apple Pencil charge, swipe from left to right on the Home screen and swipe down to the **Batteries** section (and also view the level of charge for the iPad).

BATTERIES	
iPad Pro	38% ⚡
Apple Pencil	30%

Smart Keyboard

Although the virtual keyboard on the iPad (see Chapter Four for details) is excellent for text and data inputting, or shorter pieces of writing, it is not ideal for longer items such as writing a vacation journal or a family history. To overcome this, the Apple Smart Keyboard has been introduced for use with the iPad Pro. It is a fully-functioning external keyboard that also doubles as a cover for the iPad Pro. The Smart Keyboard can be connected with the Smart connector that matches the one on the body of the iPad Pro.

Smart Keyboard Shortcuts bar

When typing with the Smart Keyboard, the same Shortcuts bar is available as with the virtual keyboard, specific to the current app.

Tap on an item on the Shortcuts bar to access it.

Smart Keyboard shortcuts

Some of the keyboard shortcuts that can be performed on the Smart Keyboard are:

- **Command (cmd) + H** – return to Home screen.

- **Command + Tab** – access the App Switcher bar, in the middle of the screen. Press the Tab button to move through the apps in the App Switcher. Stop at the app you want to open.

- **Command + spacebar** – access the Spotlight Search.

- **Press and hold Command** – a list of Smart Keyboard shortcuts in specific apps.

- **Globe key** – access available keyboards, including the emoji keyboard for adding emoji icons to text.

If a Smart Keyboard is not used with the iPad Pro, the virtual one will be available instead.

The Smart Keyboard also supports standard keyboard shortcuts such as:

Command + C – Copy.

Command + V – Paste.

Command + X – Cut.

Command + Z – Undo.

Command + B – Adds bold to selected text.

Command + I – Adds italics to selected text.

Command + U – Adds underline to selected text.

Before you Switch On

The external controls for the iPad are simple. Three of them are situated at the top of the iPad and the other is in the middle, at the bottom. There are also two cameras, one on the front and one on the back of the iPad.

Controls

The controls at the top of the iPad are:

On/Off button.

Cameras. One is located on the back, underneath the On/Off button and one on the front, at the top.

Volume Up and **Down** buttons.

Don't forget

To turn on the iPad, press and hold the **On/Off** button for a few seconds. It can also be used to Sleep the iPad or Wake it from the Sleep state, by pressing it once.

Home button. Press this once to wake up the iPad or return to the Home screen at any point.

Speakers. The speakers are located on the bottom edge of the iPad:

Lightning connector. Connect the Lightning connector here to charge the iPad, or connect it to another computer.

Hot tip

If your iPad ever freezes, or if something is not working properly, it can be rebooted by holding down the **Home** button and the **On/Off** button for 10 seconds and then turning it on again by pressing and holding the **On/Off** button.

Getting Started

To start using the iPad, hold down the On/Off button for a few seconds. Initially, there will be a series of setup screens to move through before you can use the iPad. These include the following options (a lot of these can be skipped during setup and accessed later from the **Settings** app):

- **Language**. Select the language you want to use.

- **Country**. Select the country in which you are located.

- **Wi-Fi network**. Select a Wi-Fi network to connect to the internet. If you are at home, this will be your own Wi-Fi network, if available. If you are at a Wi-Fi hotspot then this will appear on your network list.

- **Touch ID**. Use this on compatible models to create a Touch ID for unlocking your iPad, using a fingerprint.

- **Create Passcode**. This can be used to create a numerical passcode for unlocking your iPad.

- **Apps and Data (iCloud, iTunes, or new)**. This can be used to set up your iPad using an existing iCloud or iTunes backup, or as a new device.

- **Apple ID and iCloud**. An Apple ID can be set up to create an iCloud account for backing up content and sharing it with other family members, using the Family Sharing service, and also access the full range of services for the iTunes or the App Stores, Messages and iBooks.

- **Location Services**. This determines whether your iPad can use your geographical location for apps that use this type of information (such as Maps).

- **Siri.** This can be used to set up Siri, the digital voice assistant, ready for use.

- **iPad and App Analytics**. This allows details about your iPad and its apps to be sent to Apple and developers.

- **Start using**. Once the setup process has been completed, you can start using your iPad.

If you have another Apple mobile device, such as an iPhone, it can be used to transfer settings directly to your iPad, by holding next to the iPad. This is known as Quick Start, and is a new feature in iOS 11.

An iTunes backup is done by connecting the iPad to a Mac computer.

For details about obtaining an Apple ID, see page 99.

For more information about using iCloud, see pages 58-60.

iOS 11 is the new operating system for the iPad.

iOS 11 is not compatible with some older models of iPad but can be run on: iPad Mini 2 and later; iPad 5th generation and later; iPad Air and later; and all models of iPad Pro.

To check the version of the iOS, look in **Settings** > **General** > **Software Update**.

About iOS 11

iOS 11 is the latest version of the operating system for Apple's mobile devices including the iPad, the iPhone and the iPod Touch.

iOS 11 further enhances the user experience for which the mobile operating system is renowned. This includes:

- An enhanced Dock that can be accessed from anywhere, includes more apps, and displays recently-used apps.

- A newly-designed App Switcher, which also includes the redesigned Control Center. This enables currently-opened apps and the Control Center to be viewed at the same time.

- Improvements to multitasking, so that Slide Over and Split View have been enhanced to make it easier to switch between apps and also work with two apps at the same time.

- The introduction of Drag and Drop, so that some items can be dragged from one app and copied into another app by dropping them there.

- The new Files app that can be used for organizing and accessing documents, including those held in separate online storage services such as Dropbox and Google Drive. Items in the Files app can then also be copied between compatible apps on the iPad.

- A newly-designed virtual keyboard that enables text, numbers and symbols to be entered from a single keyboard, without having to toggle between others.

Home Screen

Once you have completed the setup process you will see the Home screen of the iPad. This contains the built-in apps:

At the bottom of the screen are five apps that appear by default in the Dock area (left-hand side) and recently-accessed apps (right-hand side).

Rotate the iPad, and the orientation changes automatically.

There are 27 different default wallpaper backgrounds for iOS 11 on the iPad. These can be found in **Settings** > **Wallpaper**. The options are: **Dynamic**, which means that they appear to move independently from the app icons when you tilt the iPad; and **Stills**, which are static images; and you can also use your own pictures from the Photos app. The examples used in this book are from the Dynamic range.

Items on the Dock can be removed and new ones can be added. For more details, see pages 24-25.

Home Button

The Home button, located at the bottom-middle of the iPad, can be used to perform a number of tasks:

Hot tip

Pinch together with thumb and four fingers on the screen to return to the Home screen from any open app.

 1 Click once on the **Home** button to return to the Home screen at any point

2 Double-click on the **Home** button to access the **App Switcher** window. This shows the most recently-used and open apps, and also the Control Center

Don't forget

For more details about the App Switcher, see page 26.

3 Press and hold on the **Home** button to access Siri, the voice assistant function

Don't forget

For more information about using the iPad search facilities, see pages 42-45.

Go ahead, I'm listening...

Opening Items

All apps on your iPad can be opened with minimum fuss and effort:

 1 Tap once on an icon to open the app

 2 The app opens at its own Home screen

For details about closing items, see page 27.

 3 Click once on the **Home** button to return to the main iPad Home screen

 4 From the App Switcher window, swipe between apps and tap on one to open it directly

Charging your iPad

The iPad comes with a Lightning connector to USB Cable and a USB Power Adapter, for charging the iPad:

Don't forget

iPads that can run iOS 11 only have Lightning connectors; none of them have the older 30-pin adapter.

 1 Connect the USB end of the Lightning connector to the Power Adapter

2 Connect the other end of the Lightning connector to the iPad

Hot tip

If you have older accessories with Dock connector points, you can buy a Lightning to 30-pin adapter so that you can still use them with a fourth generation (and later) iPad.

3 Plug in the Power Adapter

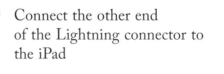

The iPad can also be charged by connecting it with the Lightning connector to another computer.

2 Around your iPad

Once you have turned on your iPad you will want to start using it as soon as possible. This chapter shows how to do this, with details about settings; navigation; multitasking options; moving documents using Drag and Drop; accessibility features; and the digital voice assistant, Siri.

iPad Settings

The Settings app should probably be explored first, as it controls settings for the appearance of the iPad and the way it and its apps operate:

The Settings are listed down the left-hand side and their options are shown on the right-hand side.

- **Apple ID and iCloud**. This contains settings for items that are to be saved to the online iCloud service (see pages 58-61).

- **Airplane Mode**. This can be used while on an airplane.

- **Wi-Fi**. This enables you to select a wireless network.

- **Bluetooth**. Turn this On to connect Bluetooth devices.

- **Notifications**. This determines how the Notification Center operates (see pages 133-134).

- **Control Center**. This determines how the Control Center operates (see pages 28-31).

- **Do Not Disturb**. Use this to specify times when you do not want to receive audio alerts or FaceTime video calls.

- **General**. This contains a number of options for how the iPad operates. This is one of the most useful settings.

- **Display & Brightness**. This can be used to set the screen brightness, text size and bold text.

- **Wallpaper**. To change the iPad's wallpaper, tap once on the **Choose a New Wallpaper** option in the Wallpaper settings and select one of the options.

- **Sounds**. This has options for setting sounds for alerts.

- **Siri & Search**. Options for turning on the digital voice assistant, and settings such as language and voice style.

- **Touch ID & Passcode**. This has options for creating a unique fingerprint ID for unlocking your iPad (see pages 48-49) and also using Apple Pay (see page 122).

- **Battery**. This shows the battery usage of specific apps and can show the battery level in the status bar.

If a Settings option has an On/Off button next to it, this can be changed by swiping the button to either the left or right. Green indicates that the option is **On**.

- **Privacy**. This can be used to activate Location Services so that your location can be used by specific apps.

- **iTunes & App Store**. This can be used to specify download options for the iTunes and App Stores.

- **Wallet & Apple Pay**. This can be used to set up Apple Pay so that you can pay for online items using your iPad (see page 122 for details).

- **Accounts & Passwords**. This contains options for managing website passwords and adding online accounts, such as Google, for email and more.

- **Mail, Contacts, Calendars**. These are three separate settings, with options for how these three apps operate.

- **Notes**. This contains options for creating and storing notes.

- **Reminders**. This has an option for syncing your reminders with other Apple devices, covering a period of time.

- **Messages**. This contains many options for using the Messages app for sending text messages.

- **FaceTime**. This is used to turn video calling On or Off.

- **Maps**. This contains options for displaying distances and is the default method for displaying directions.

- **Safari**. This has settings for the Safari web browser.

- **News**. Determines how the News app displays items.

- **Music, Videos and Photos**. These are three separate settings for managing your digital content on the iPad.

- **Camera**. This has options for viewing and editing photos and uploading them to iCloud.

- **iBooks**. Includes options for reading books in the iBooks app, including Auto-hyphenation and using bookmarks.

- **Podcasts**. Use this for options for how podcasts are downloaded and synced to your iPad.

If you have an iPad with 3G/4G connectivity, there will also be a setting for Cellular.

Tap the arrow to see additional options:

General	
About	
Software Update	

Tap once here to move back to the previous page for the selected setting:

‹ General

Name

23

The Dock has been enhanced in iOS 11.

Hot tip

Just above the Dock is a line of small dots. These indicate how many Home screens of content there are on the iPad. Tap on one of the dots to go to that Home screen, or swipe to the left or right to move between them. The white dot indicates the position of the current Home screen being viewed.

Don't forget

The functionality of open apps on other Apple devices is known as **Handoff** and can be turned On or Off in **Settings** > **General** > **Handoff**.

Using the Dock

The Dock is an element that has been part of the iPad and iOS since it was introduced. Previously, it consisted of four to six apps at the bottom of the screen. In iOS 11, the Dock has undergone its most significant enhancement in its history. The Dock now has two sections: the standard Dock area for your most frequently-used apps; and a collection of recently used apps, or those open on other iOS devices.

Elements of the Dock

Standard apps (by default these are Messages, Safari, Music, Mail and Files) are displayed on the left-hand side.

Dynamic items that change each time a new app is opened, or certain apps opened on another iOS device, are displayed on the right-hand side.

If a compatible app is open on another Apple device, i.e. an iPhone, this label appears in the right-hand corner. Tap on the app to open the same item as it is displaying on the other Apple device. Apps that

operate in this way are those linked through iCloud, and include the web browser Safari, Mail, Messages, Reminders, Calendar, Contacts and Notes.

Adding and removing Dock items

The default items on the Dock can be removed and other apps added, as required. To do this:

 Press on an item on the Dock and drag it onto the main area of the Home screen

 Repeat the process for an app on the Home screen to drag it onto the Dock

Accessing the Dock

In iOS 11 the Dock can be accessed from any app, not just from the Home screen. To do this:

 From within any app, swipe up once from the bottom of the screen to access the Dock

Don't forget

Up to 12 apps can be added to the left-hand side of the Dock. However, this reduces the size at which the apps' icons appear. There are only ever three items on the right-hand side of the Dock, and this changes each time a new app is opened or accessed (unless it is already in the main area of the Dock).

Hot tip

Press the Home button once to return to the Home screen, displaying the Dock, from any app.

The App Switcher window has been enhanced in iOS 11.

Press the Home button once to exit the App Switcher and return to the app you were using immediately before accessing the App Switcher.

App Switcher Window

The App Switcher feature in iOS 11 performs a number of shortcuts and useful tasks:

- It shows open apps and enables you to move between these and access them by tapping once on the required item.

- It displays the Control Center.

- It enables apps to be closed (see next page).

Accessing App Switcher

The App Switcher window can be accessed from any screen on your iPad, as follows:

1 Double-click on the **Home** button, or

2 From any Home screen, swipe up to access the App Switcher window, containing the Control Center at the right-hand side

3 From any app, swipe up to access the Dock as on page 25, and swipe up again to access the App Switcher window

Closing Items

The iPad deals with open apps very efficiently. They rarely interact with other apps, which increases security and also means that they can be open in the background, without using up a significant amount of processing power, in a state of semi-hibernation until they are needed. Because of this, it is not essential to close apps when you move to something else. However, you may want to close apps if you feel you have too many open or if one stops working. To do this:

Don't forget

When you switch from one app to another, the first one stays open in the background. You can go back to it by accessing it from the App Switcher window or the Home screen.

1 Access the App Switcher window. The currently-open apps are displayed

2 Press and hold on an app and swipe it to the top of the screen to close it. This does not remove it from the iPad and it can be opened again in the usual way

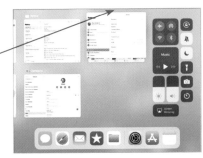

Don't forget

Swipe left and right in the App Switcher window to view all of the open apps.

3 The app is removed from its position in the App Switcher window

The Control Center has been enhanced in iOS 11.

Swipe up once from the bottom of the Lock screen to access the Control Center on its own, without the App Switcher.

AirDrop is the functionality for sharing items wirelessly between compatible devices. Tap once on the **AirDrop** button in the Control Center and specify whether you want to share with **Contacts Only** or **Everyone**. Once AirDrop is set up, you can use the **Share** button in compatible apps to share items such as photos with any other AirDrop users in the vicinity.

Using the Control Center

The Control Center is a panel containing commonly-used options within the **Settings** app. In iOS 11 it is part of the App Switcher, and is an excellent option for when you do not want to have to go into Settings.

Accessing the Control Center

The Control Center can be accessed from any screen within iOS 11 and it can also be accessed from the Lock screen:

 Swipe up once from the bottom of the Home screen, or swipe up twice from the bottom of any app screen, to access the App Switcher window, containing the Control Center panel at the right-hand side

Control Center functionality

The Control Panel contains items that have differing format and functionality. To access these:

 Press on the folder of four icons to access the **Airplane Mode**, **AirDrop**, **Wi-Fi** and **Bluetooth** options

2 Press on the Music button to expand the options for music controls, including playing or pausing items and changing the volume. Tap once on this icon to send music from your iPad to other compatible devices, such AirPod headphones or HomePods; Apple's wireless speakers

When Airplane mode is activated, the network and wireless connectivity on the iPad is disabled. However, it can still be used for functions such as playing music or reading books.

29

3 Tap once on individual buttons to turn items On or Off (they change color depending on their state)

Hot tip

Press on the brightness and volume buttons to access panels that allow greater precision by dragging on their respective bars.

4 Drag on these items to increase or decrease the screen brightness and the volume

Hot tip

Press on the Clock and the Flashlight buttons to access bars for setting a timer and the strength of the flashlight. Drag on the bars to alter them.

Don't forget

The Control Center also has a Screen Mirroring option, for displaying what is on the iPad on a compatible High-Definition TV.

...cont'd

Control Center options

Access items in the Control Center as follows:

- Tap once on this button to turn **Airplane mode** On or Off.

- Tap once on this button to activate **AirDrop** for sharing items with other AirDrop users.

- Tap once on this button to turn **Wi-Fi** On or Off.

- Tap once on this button to turn **Bluetooth** On or Off.

- Tap once on this button to **Lock** or **Unlock** screen rotation. If it is locked, the screen will not change when you change the orientation of your iPad.

- Tap once on this button to **Mute** all sounds.

- Tap once on this button to turn **Do Not Disturb** mode On or Off.

- Tap once on this button to turn on the **Flashlight**. Press on the button to change the intensity of the flashlight.

- Tap once on this button to access the **Clock**, including a stopwatch and timer. Press on the button to access a scale for creating reminders.

- Tap once on this button to open the **Camera** app. Press on the button to access options for taking a selfie (a self-portrait), recording a video, recording a slow-motion video and taking a standard photo.

Customizing the Control Center

The items in the Control Center can be customized so that items can be added or removed. To do this:

1 Tap once on the **Settings** app

2 Tap once on the **Control Center** tab

Control Center

3 Tap once on the **Customize Controls** button

Customize Controls

Customizing the Control Center is a new feature in iOS 11.

4 The items currently in the Control Center are shown at the top of the window; those that can be added are below them. Tap once on a red icon to remove an existing item, or tap once on a green icon to add new items to the Control Center

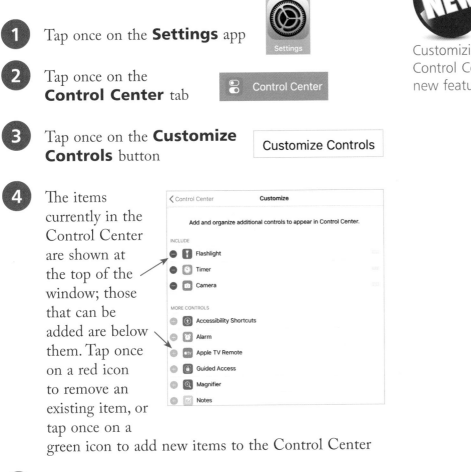

5 Items that are added in Step 4 are included in the Control Center, and can be accessed from here

Navigating Around

Much of the navigation on the iPad is done with Multitasking Gestures, which are combinations of tapping, swiping and pinching gestures that can be used to view items such as web pages, photos, maps and documents.

Swiping between screens
Once you have added more apps to your iPad they will start to fill up more screens. To move between these:

Swipe left or right with one or two fingers.

Returning to the Home screen
Pinch together with thumb and four fingers to return to the Home screen from any open app.

Swiping up and down
Swipe up and down with one finger to move up or down web pages, photos, maps or documents. The content moves in the opposite direction of the swipe; i.e. if you swipe up, the page will move down, and vice versa.

Don't forget

Multitasking Gestures and Multitouch Gestures are the same, and the terms are interchangeable.

Don't forget

You can also move between different screens by tapping once on one of the small white dots in the middle of the screen above the Dock.

Don't forget

You can also return to the Home screen by clicking once on the Home button.

Hot tip

The faster you swipe on the screen, the faster the screen moves up or down.

Tapping and zooming

Double-tap with one finger to zoom in on a web page, photo, map or document. Double-tap with one finger to return to the original view.

Pinching and swiping

Swipe outwards with thumb and forefinger to zoom in on a web page, photo, map or document.

Pinch together with thumb and forefinger to zoom back out on a web page, photo, map or document.

Don't forget

Swiping outwards with thumb and forefinger enables you to zoom in on an item to a greater degree than double-tapping with one finger.

More gestures

- Swipe left or right with four or five fingers to move between open apps.

- Drag with two or three fingers to move a web page, photo, map or document.

- Press and swipe down on any free area on the Home screen to access the Spotlight Search box.

- Swipe left or right with one finger to move between full-size photos in the Photos app.

- Tap once on a photo thumbnail with one finger to enlarge it to full screen within the Photos app.

- Drag up from the bottom of the Home screen to access the Control Center.

- Drag down at the top-middle of the iPad to view current notifications in the Notification Center.

Hot tip

The Multitasking Gestures involving four or five fingers can be turned On or Off in the **General** section of the **Settings** app (**Settings** > **General** > **Multitasking & Dock**).

Multitasking Screens

The iPad has evolved from being an internet-enabled communication and entertainment device into something that is now a genuine productivity device. With iOS 11, productivity options are enhanced with the further development of Slide Over and Split View (only with certain models of iPad). These are options that enable two apps to be viewed and worked with, within a single screen. This means it is much easier to perform several tasks without having to constantly switch between apps.

Slide Over

Slide Over is an option that is available on the iPad, iPad Pro, iPad Mini 2 (and later) and iPad Air (and later). It enables you to activate a second app as a floating bar while another app is open at full screen below it. To do this:

The Slide Over and Split View functions have been enhanced in iOS 11.

1 Open the first app that you want to use

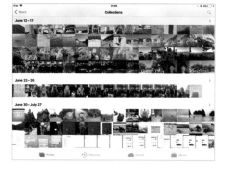

Hot tip

For apps that you will use regularly in Slide Over and Split View, add them to the main area of the Dock so that they are always available in Step 3.

2 Swipe up from the bottom of the screen to access the Dock

3 Press and hold on an app on the Dock and drag it over the first app

4 Release the second app. Regardless of where it is positioned, it will snap to the right-hand side of the screen as a floating bar over the first app

5 Press and hold on this button to drag the Slide Over panel to the left-hand side of the screen (or swipe on the button, from right to left)

6 The two apps can be used independently of each other, e.g. move through different views in Photos and then move through your Twitter feed

7 Swipe up from the bottom of the screen to access the Dock. Tap once on another app to open it as the main panel. Drag another app and release it over the first one to add it as the Slide Over panel

Don't forget

If the main app is exited, e.g. by going back to the Home screen, the Slide Over panel will still be available when you access the main app again, by swiping inwards from the right-hand edge of the screen.

35

...cont'd

Split View

On the iPad Pro and iPad Air 2 (and later) the concept of Slide Over is taken one step further by Split View: the second item can become a fixed item, which can then be resized so that it has equal prominence to the first app. To do this:

Not all third-party apps support Split View, but the number is growing.

1 Open the first app that you want to use

2 Swipe up from the bottom of the screen to access the Dock

3 Press and hold on an app on the Dock and drag it to the right-hand or left-hand side of the screen, and release the app when a dark bar appears below it

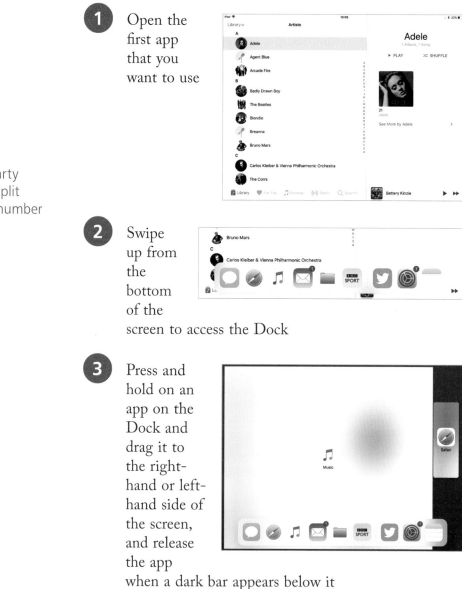

4 Initially, the app in Split View takes up 30% of the screen and can be used independently of the other app

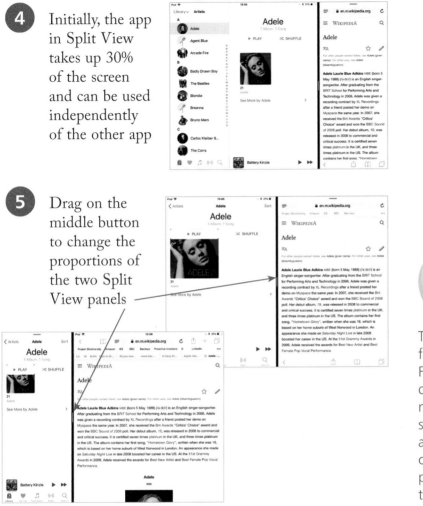

5 Drag on the middle button to change the proportions of the two Split View panels

Don't forget

The Picture-in-Picture function enables a FaceTime video, or other video, to be minimized on the screen but remain active so that you can still view it and perform other tasks at the same time.

6 Press and hold on the middle button and drag it away from the right-hand (or left-hand) edge of the screen to close one of the Split View apps

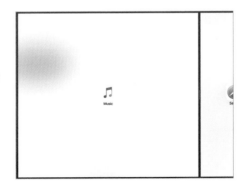

Drag and Drop is a new feature in iOS 11 on the iPad.

For more information about the different views in the Photos app, see page 154.

Since Drag and Drop is a new feature in iOS 11 it only works with a limited number of apps, at the time of printing. However, this will increase as more third-party apps are produced with support for Drag and Drop.

Drag and Drop

With iOS 11 it is now possible to perform a range of drag-and-drop tasks, to make it easier to move and share items:

- Dragging photos into an email or a document
- Dragging links for opening web pages
- Dragging files from a file manager into another app

Dragging photos

Photos can be dragged from the Photos app to the Notes, Mail and Messages apps for sending to family or friends:

1 Open the **Photos** app and drag a second app into Split View, as shown on page 36

2 Navigate to the required photo, in Moments view, and press and hold on it. Drag the photo into the app on the right-hand side (a green **+** icon appears, to indicate that the app supports drag-and-drop functionality)

3 The photo is added to the second app

Dragging text

Text can be dragged into different locations, and this is a good way to copy text between apps. To do this:

1 Open two apps in Split View, as shown on page 36

2 Select a piece of text in an app such as Notes

Thailand
Singapore
Malaysia
Vietnam
Cambodia

3 Press on the piece of text and drag it into the other app (a green **+** icon appears, to indicate that the app supports drag-and-drop functionality)

Cancel   **Places to visit**

To: Eilidh

Cc/Bcc, From: nickvandome@me.com

Subject: **Places to visit**

Here are the ideas I had:

Thailand
Singapore
Malaysia
Vietnam
Cambodia

4 The text is added to the second app

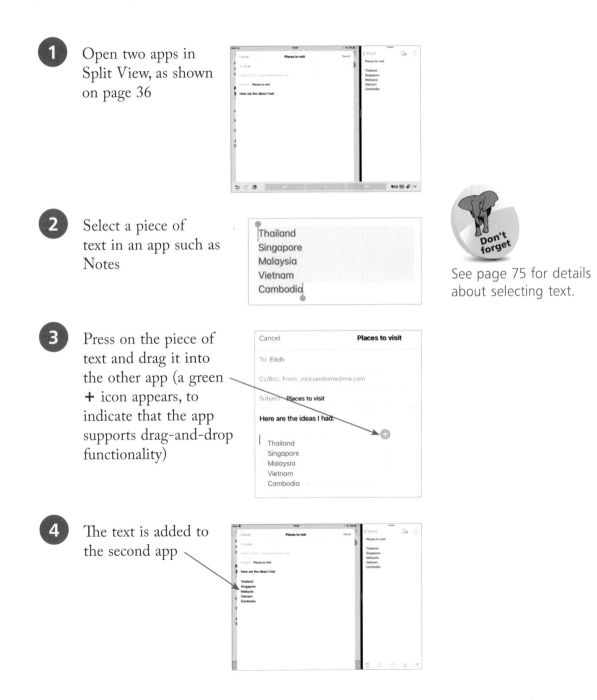

See page 75 for details about selecting text.

Don't forget

...cont'd

Dragging links

News and web headlines and links can be dragged into different locations, and this is a useful way to create dynamic links. When the link is tapped on in the app it is copied to, the relevant item opens in its parent app:

Dragging headlines is a good way to share them with family and friends – drag the headline into an app such as Mail or Messages, and the recipient will be able to access the item from the headline link.

 Open two apps in Split View, as shown on page 36 (one of them should be the News app or the Safari web browser)

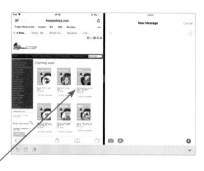

 Press on a headline, or a link, and drag it into the second app (a green **+** icon appears, to indicate that the app supports drag-and-drop functionality)

3 The link is added to the second app

4 Tap on the link to open it in its parent app, e.g. if it was copied from Safari, this is where the link will open

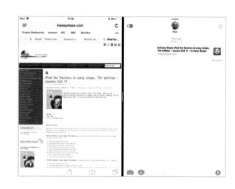

Dragging files

Dragging and dropping can also be used to move files using the Files app. This can be a good way to move complete documents and share them with other people. To do this:

1 Open the **Files** app

2 Access the Dock and open a second app in Split View

See pages 62-63 for more details about using the Files app.

3 Press and hold on one of the documents in the Files app and drag it into the second app

4 The document is copied to the second app

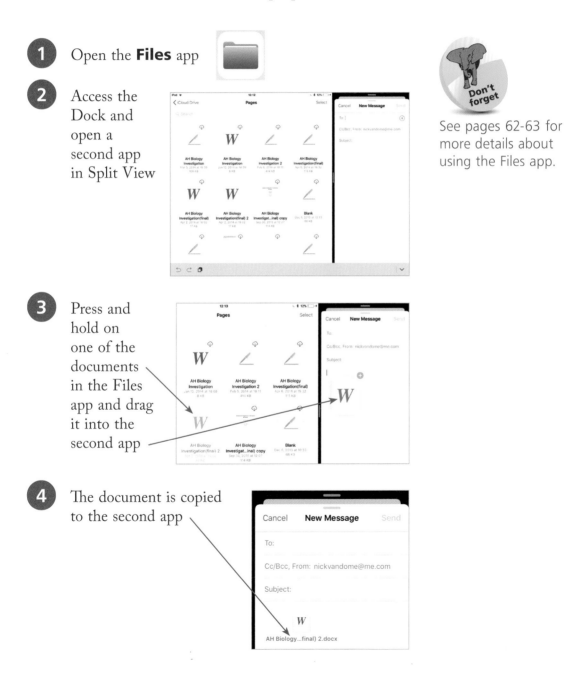

Finding Things with Siri

Siri is the iPad voice assistant that provides answers to a variety of questions, by looking within your iPad and also with the use of web services. You can ask Siri questions relating to the apps on your iPad and also general questions, such as weather conditions around the world, or sports results. Initially, Siri can be set up within the **Settings** app:

Siri can be used to open any of the built-in iPad apps, simply by saying, for example: "**Open Photos**".

1 Tap once on the **Siri & Search** option

Turn **On** the **Listen for "Hey Siri"** button in the first Step 2 to activate Siri just by saying this phrase, without having to press the Home button.

2 Tap once on the options to select a language, set voice feedback and allow access to your details (Siri can also be set up when you first start to use your iPad)

Questioning Siri

Once you have set up Siri, you can start putting it to work with your queries. To do this:

Tap once on this button at the bottom of the Siri window to ask another question of Siri.

1 Hold down the **Home** button until the Siri window appears

2 To find something within your iPad apps, make a request such as **Show me my calendar**

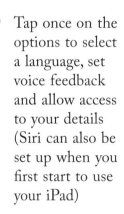

...cont'd

Siri can also find information from across the web and related web services:

 Siri can provide sports results for certain sports in certain countries, such as in response to the request **Show the latest Red Sox score**

Don't forget

Siri can be used with a range of Apple and specific third-party apps. For instance, you can ask it to find specific photos in the Photos app, send a message to someone with the Messages app, and even book restaurants and taxis with compatible apps.

43

 Global weather reports are another of Siri's strong points, and it can provide forecasts in response to the question **What is the weather like in Hanoi?**

At the time of printing, Siri can be used to translate English words or phrases into French, German, Italian, Mandarin Chinese and Spanish. This is a new feature in iOS 11.

3 However, even Siri's knowledge is limited and if there is a subject it does not recognize, it will provide details from Wikipedia or the web instead

Searching with Spotlight

Siri can be used to search for items on your iPad and you can also use the built-in search engine, Spotlight.

Accessing Spotlight

To access and use the Spotlight Search box:

Don't forget

To return to the Home screen from the Spotlight Search page, press the **Home** button once.

 1 Swipe downwards on any free area of the Home screen. This also activates the keyboard. Enter the search keywords into the Search box at the top of the window, and results will display automatically

 2 As keywords are entered into the Spotlight Search box, the options are shown underneath. The options become more defined as more words are entered

3 For items such as people, there will be matches from the items in which they appear in apps across your iPad, including Mail, Notes and Contacts

4 For items such as nearby attractions or restaurants, any matches will appear at the top of the Spotlight window. Tap once on a result to view its details and its location in Maps, from where you can also go to its website (if there is one)

Hot tip

Enter the name of an app into the Spotlight Search box, and tap on the result to launch the app from here.

5 Swipe to the bottom of the Spotlight window to use the **Search Web**, **Search App Store** and **Search Maps** options for the required item

Using the Lock Screen

To save power, it is possible to set your iPad screen to lock automatically. This is the equivalent of the Sleep option on a traditional computer. To do this:

Don't forget

The screen can also be locked by pressing once on the On/Off button at the top of the iPad.

1 Tap once on the **Settings** app

Don't forget

Auto-locking the screen does not prevent other people from accessing your iPad. If you want to prevent anyone else having access, it can be locked with a passcode. See page 48 for details.

2 Tap once on the **Display & Brightness** tab

AA   Display & Brightness

3 Tap once on the **Auto-Lock** option

Auto-Lock	2 Minutes >

4 Select a length of time until the iPad is locked automatically, when it is not being used

< Display & Brightness   **Auto-Lock**

2 Minutes	✓
5 Minutes	
10 Minutes	
15 Minutes	
Never	

5 When the iPad is locked, press the **Home** button to exit the Lock screen. Swipe from left to right to view the Lock screen widgets (see the next page)

Working with the Lock screen

In addition to locking the iPad, the Lock screen can also be used to display a range of information without having to unlock the iPad. This includes real-time information from widgets, which can be customized on the Lock screen.

 1 Swipe from left to right on the Lock screen to access the widgets, which are displayed in one column

Hot tip

Swipe up on the window in Step 3 to view items that can be added to the Lock screen. Tap once on the green buttons to add items.

2 Swipe up the page and tap once on the **Edit** button to manage the Lock screen items

`Edit`

3 Tap once on a red button next to one of the items in the left or right columns to select a widget for removal

Hot tip

Press and hold on this button, and drag the item up or down to change the order in which it appears on the Lock screen.

4 Tap once on the **Remove** button to remove the item from the Lock screen

Locking and Unlocking an iPad

Adding a passcode

When the iPad is locked, i.e. the Lock screen is displayed, it can be unlocked simply by pressing the **Home** button. However, this is not secure, as anyone could unlock the iPad. A better option is to add a numerical passcode. To do this:

Hot tip

Notifications can be displayed on the iPad's Lock screen. This can be activated by going to **Settings** > **Notifications** > **Show Previews** and then selecting **Always**.

Don't forget

Once the passcode has been set, tap on the **Require Passcode** button in the Touch ID & Passcode section to specify when the passcode is activated. The best option is **Immediately**, otherwise someone else could access your iPad before the passcode is activated.

 1 Select **Settings** > **Touch ID & Passcode**

2 Tap once on the **Turn Passcode On** button

Turn Passcode On

3 Enter a six-digit passcode. This can be used to unlock your iPad from the Lock screen. Confirm the passcode on the next screen

4 The passcode is now required on the Lock screen whenever the iPad is locked

Require Passcode   Immediately >

Fingerprint sensor with Touch ID

For greater security, the Home button can be used as a fingerprint sensor to unlock your iPad with the unique fingerprint that has set it up. (A passcode also has to be set up in case the Touch ID does not work.) To do this:

 Select **Settings** > **Touch ID & Passcode**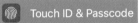

 Create a passcode as shown on page 48 (this is required if the fingerprint sensor is unavailable for any reason)

3 Drag the **iPad Unlock** button to **On** and tap once on the **Add a Fingerprint...** link. This presents a screen for creating your Touch ID

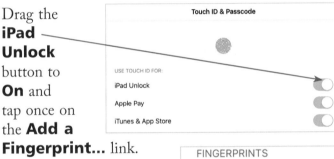

Touch ID & Passcode

USE TOUCH ID FOR:

iPad Unlock

Apple Pay

iTunes & App Store

FINGERPRINTS

Add a Fingerprint...

4 Place your finger on the Home button several times to create the Touch ID. This will include capturing the edges of your finger. The screens move automatically after each part is captured, and the fingerprint icon turns red. Complete the Touch ID wizard to create a unique fingerprint for unlocking your iPad

Place Your Finger

Lift and rest your finger on the Home button repeatedly.

Hot tip

A Touch ID and passcode can be used to set up Apple Pay, to be used for paying for items on the web. For more details, see page 122.

49

Don't forget

The fingerprint sensor is very effective, although it may take a bit of practice until you can get the right position for your finger to unlock the iPad first time, every time. It can only be unlocked with the same finger that created the Touch ID in Step 4. Additional fingerprints can also be set up. The Touch ID may not work if your finger is wet.

Don't forget

If your iOS software is up-to-date, there is a message to this effect in the **Software Update** window.

Hot tip

It is always worth updating the iOS to keep up-to-date with fixes. Also, app developers update their products to use the latest iOS features.

Hot tip

Software can also be updated by connecting your iPad to a Mac computer, using the Lightning/USB cable, and opening iTunes. Access the iPad within iTunes, click on the **Summary** tab in the left-hand panel, and click on the **Check for Updates** button.

Updating Software

The operating system that powers the iPad is known as iOS. This is a mobile-computing operating system, and it is also used on the iPhone and the iPod Touch. The latest version is iOS 11. Periodically, there are updates to the iOS to fix bugs and add new features. These can be downloaded to your iPad once they are released:

1 Tap once on the **Settings** app

2 Tap on the **General** tab

3 Tap on the **Software Update** option

> Software Update >

4 If there is an update available it will be displayed here, with details of what is contained within it, from the **Learn More** link

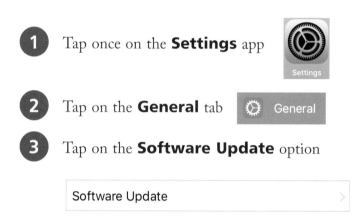

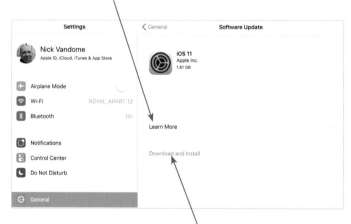

5 Tap once on the **Download and Install** link to start the download process. The iOS update will then download and install automatically

Accessibility Issues

The iPad tries to cater to as wide a range of users as possible, including those who have difficulty with vision, hearing or physical and motor issues. There are a number of settings that can help with these areas. To access the range of accessibility settings:

1 Tap once on the **Settings** app

2 Tap on the **General** tab
General

3 Tap on the **Accessibility** option
Accessibility

4 The settings for **Vision**, **Interaction**, **Hearing**, **Media** and **Learning** are displayed here:

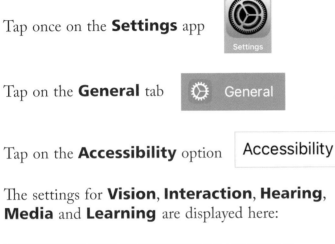

‹ General	Accessibility	
VISION		
VoiceOver	Off >
Zoom	Off >
Magnifier	Off >
Display Accommodations	Off >
Speech	>
Larger Text	Off >
Bold Text	
Button Shapes	
Increase Contrast	>
Reduce Motion	Off >
On/Off Labels	
INTERACTION		
Switch Control	Off >

Hot tip

In the Accessibility section, drag the **On/Off Labels** button to **On** to display an extra graphical symbol on the On/Off buttons, to further help identify their state.

Beware

VoiceOver works with the built-in iPad apps and some apps from the App Store, but not all of them.

Don't forget

When VoiceOver is On, tap once on an item to select it and have it spoken; double-tap to activate the item.

Hot tip

There is a wide range of options for the way VoiceOver can be used. For full details, see the Apple website at **www.apple.com/ accessibility/ios/ voiceover**

...cont'd

Vision settings

These can help anyone with impaired vision, and there are options to hear items on the screen and also for making text easier to read:

1 Tap once on the **VoiceOver** option

> VISION
>
> VoiceOver   Off >

2 Drag this button to **On** to activate the VoiceOver function. This then enables items to be spoken when you tap on them

> ‹ Accessibility   **VoiceOver**
>
> VoiceOver
>
> VoiceOver speaks items on the screen:
> • Tap once to select an item
> • Double-tap to activate the selected item
> • Swipe three fingers to scroll
>
> VoiceOver Practice

3 Select options for VoiceOver, as required

> SPEAKING RATE
>
> ⎯⎯⎯⎯⎯◯⎯⎯⎯⎯⎯
>
> Speech   >
>
> Verbosity   >

4 Tap once on the **Accessibility** button to return to the main options

 < Accessibility

5 Tap once on these options to access settings for zooming the screen, increasing text size, changing the text color on the screen, and speaking text

< General	Accessibility	
VISION		
VoiceOver		Off >
Zoom		Off >
Magnifier		Off >
Display Accommodations		Off >
Speech		>

6 Tap again on the **Accessibility** button to return to the main options after each selection

Hearing settings

These can be used to change the iPad speaker from stereo to mono. To do this:

1 Drag this button to **On** to enable **Mono Audio**

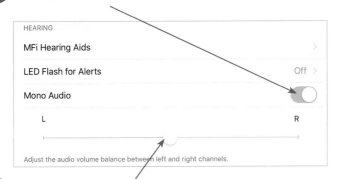

HEARING	
MFi Hearing Aids	>
LED Flash for Alerts	Off >
Mono Audio	

L   R

Adjust the audio volume balance between left and right channels.

2 Drag this button to specify whether sound comes out of the left or right speaker

Don't forget

If you turn on the **Zoom** function, you can magnify areas of the screen with a magnification window. To activate this, double-tap with three fingers. Drag with three fingers within the window to view different areas of the screen, or press and hold on the tab in the middle-bottom of the window to drag it into different positions.

53

Hot tip

The **Speak Auto-text** function (accessed from **Speech** > **Typing Feedback** in the **Vision** section) can be turned on so that auto-corrections and auto-capitalizations are automatically spoken.

...cont'd

AssistiveTouch

This can be used by anyone who has difficulty navigating around the iPad with the screen or buttons. It can be used with an external device such as a joystick, or it can be used on its own. To use AssistiveTouch (under **Interaction**):

1 Tap once on the **AssistiveTouch** option

Don't forget

The **AssistiveTouch** options make it easier for anyone with difficulties clicking the Home button, or using Multitasking Gestures.

2 Drag this button to **On** to activate the **AssistiveTouch** function

3 The AssistiveTouch icon appears on the screen and can be dragged around

4 Tap once on the AssistiveTouch icon to view its options

5 Tap once on the **Home** icon to return to the Home screen

6 Tap once on the **Custom** icon to access options for using custom gestures. Tap on the screen to minimize the AssistiveTouch options window

Custom

7 To create a custom gesture, tap once on the **Create New Gesture button** in the AssistiveTouch section

CUSTOM GESTURES

Create New Gesture...

The **AssistiveTouch** section can be used to perform Multitasking Gestures, without having to physically use the full number of fingers on the screen.

8 Drag on the screen with your required gesture (e.g. swiping with four fingers to move between open apps)

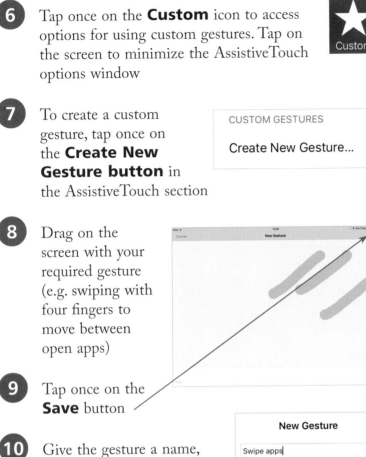

9 Tap once on the **Save** button

10 Give the gesture a name, and tap the **Save** button

New Gesture

Swipe apps

Cancel   Save

11 The gesture is added under the **Custom** section

12 Tap once on a gesture to select it. A number of black circles appear, corresponding to the number of fingers used in the gesture. Tap on one to activate the gesture

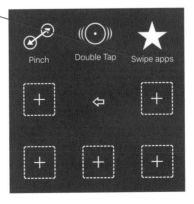

Pinch   Double Tap   Swipe apps

Tap on the **More** button in the **Device** window to select options for creating more gestures, shaking the iPad, capturing a screenshot and accessing the App Switcher window.

...cont'd

 Tap on the **Device** icon

 Tap once to activate the required function, including changing the screen rotation and adjusting the volume

Guided Access

The Guided Access option allows for certain functionality within an app to be disabled so that individual tasks can be focused on without any other distractions. To use this:

 Under the **Learning** heading, tap once on the **Guided Access** arrow

LEARNING

Guided Access

 Drag this button to **On** to activate the Guided Access functionality

 Open an app, and triple-click on the **Home** button to activate Guided Access within the app

 Circle an area on the screen to disable it (this can be any functionality within the app). Tap on the **Start** button to activate Guided Access for that area. The circled area will not function within the app

3 iCloud

This chapter shows how to use the online iCloud services for storing and sharing documents.

Living in the iCloud

iCloud is the Apple online service that performs a number of valuable functions:

It is free to register for and set up a standard iCloud account.

- It makes your content available across multiple devices. The content is stored in the iCloud and then pushed out to other iCloud-enabled devices, including the iPhone, iPod Touch and other Mac or Windows computers.

- It enables online access to your content via the iCloud website. This includes your iCloud email, Contacts, Calendar and Reminders.

- It backs up the content of your iPad.

Once you have registered for and set up iCloud, it works automatically so you do not have to worry about anything. You can activate iCloud when you first set up your iPad, or:

To access your iCloud account through the website, access www.icloud.com and enter your Apple ID details (see page 99).

1 Tap once on the **Settings** app

2 At the top of the Settings panel, tap once on the **Sign in to your iPad** option

> **Settings**
>
> Sign in to your iPad
> Set up iCloud, the App Store, and more.

3 If you already have an Apple ID, enter your details and tap once on the **Sign In** button

4 If you do not yet have an Apple ID, tap once on the **Don't have an Apple ID or forgot it?** link and follow the steps to create your Apple ID

iCloud settings

After you have set up your iCloud account you can then apply settings for how it works. Once you have done this, you will not have to worry about it again:

1 Access the **Apple ID** section in the Settings app, as shown on page 58

2 Tap once on the **iCloud** button

Tap once on the **Photos** option to access settings for storing and using your photos in iCloud.

3 Drag these buttons to **On** for items you want to be synced with iCloud. Each item is then saved and stored in the iCloud, and made available to other iCloud-enabled devices

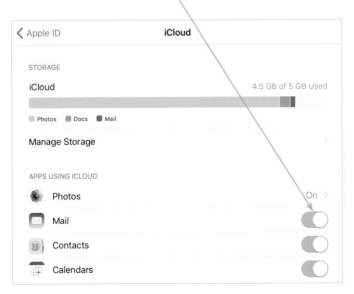

Another useful iCloud function is the iCloud Keychain (**Settings > Apple ID > iCloud > Keychain**). If this is enabled, it can keep all of your passwords and credit card information up-to-date across multiple devices and remember them when you use them on websites. The information is encrypted and controlled through your Apple ID.

...cont'd

iCloud storage & backup

To view the storage on your iCloud account:

1 Tap once on the **Manage Storage** option in Step 3 on page 59

Manage Storage

2 The amount of storage that has been used is indicated by the colored bar at the top of the window (yellow for photos, orange for documents and blue for email)

<table>
<tr><td>❮ iCloud</td><td>**iCloud Storage**</td><td></td></tr>
<tr><td>iCloud</td><td></td><td>4.5 GB of 5 GB Used</td></tr>
<tr><td colspan="3">▉ Photos ▉ Docs ▉ Mail</td></tr>
<tr><td>☁ iCloud Storage</td><td></td><td>Upgrade</td></tr>
<tr><td colspan="3">iCloud stores the most important things from your device, like photos, messages, documents, and more.</td></tr>
</table>

3 Tap once on the **Upgrade** button to increase the amount of storage (the default amount is 5GB, which is provided free of charge)

Prices are shown in local currencies.

4 Select another storage plan as required, and tap once on the **Buy** button

Back	**Upgrade iCloud Storage**	Buy
iCloud stores the most important things from your device, like photos, documents, contacts, and more, so they're always available, even if you lose your device.		
CURRENT PLAN		
5GB	Free	
CHOOSE UPGRADE		
By selecting a new plan and tapping Buy, you will be charged the amount below now and each month until you change or cancel your plan.		
50GB	£0.79 a month	✓
200GB	£2.49 a month Can be shared with your family	
2TB	£6.99 a month Can be shared with your family	

About the iCloud Drive

One of the options in the iCloud section is for the iCloud Drive. This can be used to store documents so that you can use them on any other Apple devices that you have, such as an iPhone or a MacBook. With iCloud Drive (and the Files app) you can start work on a document on one device and continue on another device from where you left off.

1 Tap once on the **Apple ID** tab of the Settings app

Nick Vandome
Apple ID, iCloud, iTunes & App Store

2 Tap once on the **iCloud** button

☁ iCloud

3 By default, the iCloud Drive is set to **Off**

☁ iCloud Drive

4 Slide the **iCloud Drive** button to green to turn it **On**

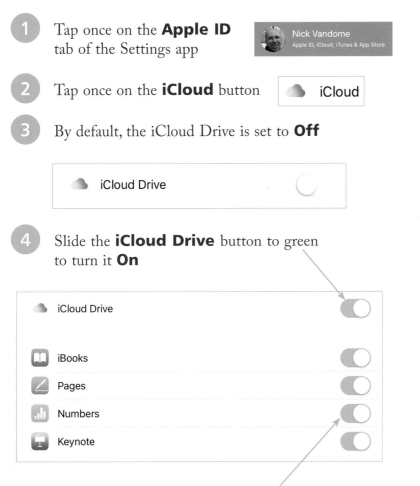

61

Beware

To use iCloud Drive effectively, all devices have to be using iOS 8 (or later) for mobile devices, or OS X Yosemite (or later) for desktop or laptop Mac computers. Also, iCloud Drive-compatible apps (such as Pages, Numbers and Keynote) should be updated to their latest versions via the App Store.

5 Drag the buttons **On** for the apps that you want to activate for syncing files with iCloud Drive. Content that you create with these apps will be stored in the iCloud Drive and be available within the same apps on other devices

Files App

Once the iCloud Drive has been activated within the iCloud Settings, documents can be viewed and accessed using the Files app. This can be used to store documents and files that have been created on the iPad and also other online storage services, such as Dropbox and Google Drive. To start using the Files app:

The Files app is a new feature in iOS 11 on the iPad.

By default, the Files app is on the Dock.

Tap once on this button on the top toolbar to add a new folder to the top level of the Files app, or within any of the existing folders.

1 Tap once on the **Files** app

2 The Files app window shows items that are stored there, as specified by the selection in Step 5 on page 61

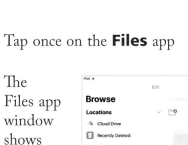

3 Tap once on the **iCloud Drive** button and tap once on a folder to view its contents. By default, the documents are stored in the iCloud. Tap once on an item to open it and download it to your iPad

...cont'd

4   Tap once on the **Select** button on the top toolbar

Select

5   Tap once on items to select them

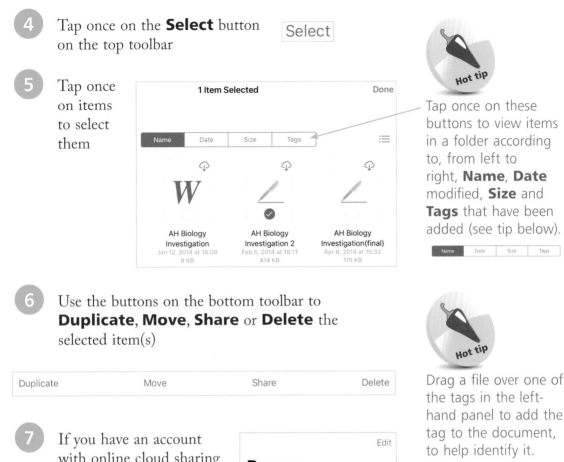

Hot tip

Tap once on these buttons to view items in a folder according to, from left to right, **Name**, **Date** modified, **Size** and **Tags** that have been added (see tip below).

6   Use the buttons on the bottom toolbar to **Duplicate**, **Move**, **Share** or **Delete** the selected item(s)

Duplicate	Move	Share	Delete

Hot tip

Drag a file over one of the tags in the left-hand panel to add the tag to the document, to help identify it.

7   If you have an account with online cloud sharing services such as Dropbox or Google Drive, these will be available via the Files app, once you have downloaded the apps from the App Store and logged into them

Don't forget

Tap once on a location other than iCloud Drive, i.e. Dropbox, to view its folder structure. Tap once on items within the folders to download them to your iPad.

8   Tap once on the **Edit** button in the previous step to show or hide the items by dragging their buttons **On** or **Off**

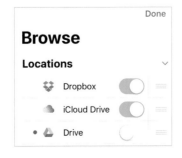

63

About Family Sharing

As everyone gets more and more digital devices, it is becoming increasingly important to be able to share content with other people, particularly family members. In iOS 11, the Family Sharing function enables you to share items that you have downloaded from the App Store, such as music and movies, with up to six other family members, as long as they have an Apple ID Account. Once this has been set up, it is also possible to share items such as family calendars and photos, and even see where family members are, on a map. To set up and start using Family Sharing:

To use Family Sharing, other family members must have an Apple device using either iOS 8 (or later) for a mobile device (iPad, iPhone or iPod Touch) or OS X Yosemite (or later) for a desktop or laptop Mac computer.

64

1 Access the **iCloud** section within the Settings app, as shown on page 59

2 Tap once on the **Set Up Family Sharing...** link

Set Up Family Sharing...

3 Tap once on the **Get Started** button

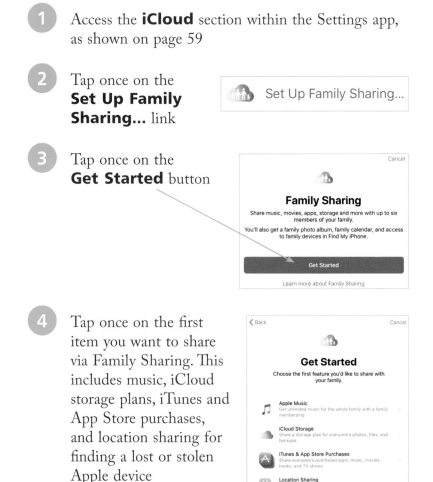

Cancel

Family Sharing

Share music, movies, apps, storage and more with up to six members of your family.

You'll also get a family photo album, family calendar, and access to family devices in Find My iPhone.

Get Started

Learn more about Family Sharing

4 Tap once on the first item you want to share via Family Sharing. This includes music, iCloud storage plans, iTunes and App Store purchases, and location sharing for finding a lost or stolen Apple device

‹ Back   Cancel

Get Started

Choose the first feature you'd like to share with your family.

♪ **Apple Music**
Get unlimited music for the whole family with a family membership.

iCloud Storage
Share a storage plan for everyone's photos, files, and backups.

Ⓐ **iTunes & App Store Purchases**
Share everyone's purchased apps, music, movies, books, and TV shows.

Location Sharing
Share your location with family members in Messages and Find My Friends.

5 Tap once on the **Continue** button again to confirm your Apple ID account for Family Sharing

Confirm Account

You will be the family organizer and will share purchases made with "nickvandome@mac.com"

Family members will be able to view and download your purchased music, movies, TV shows, books, and apps. Available content may vary by country or region.

Continue

Use a Different Account

6 If you are the organizer of Family Sharing, payments will be taken from the credit/debit card that you registered when you set up your Apple ID. Tap once on the **Continue** button to confirm this

Shared Payment

As the family organizer, your payment method (••••) will be shared with your family members.

You agree to pay for iTunes, iBooks and App Store purchases initiated by family members using this payment method and will be responsible for all the charges.

Managing family purchases

Continue

Use Different Payment

7 Once Family Sharing has been created, return to the iCloud section in the Settings app and tap once on the **Invite Via iMessage** button

Invite Family Members

Invite up to five people from your household to join your family.

Your family can also share an Apple Music membership, an iCloud storage plan, and any other family features you set up.

Learn more about Family Sharing

Invite Via iMessage

Not Now

8 Enter the name or email address of a family member, and tap once on the **Send** button

New iMessage

To: Eilidh

Nick Vandome has invited you to share purchased music, movies, TV shows, books, and apps with your family.

View Invitation

Would you like to join Family Sharing?

9 An invitation is sent to the selected person. They have to accept this before they can participate in Family Sharing

Hot tip

If children are added to Family Sharing you can specify that they have to ask permission before downloading content from the iTunes Store, the App Store or the iBooks Store. To do this, select them in the **Family Sharing** section of the **iCloud** settings and drag the **Ask To Buy** button to **On**. Each time they want to buy something you will be sent a notification asking for approval. This is a good option if grandchildren are added to the Family Sharing group.

Using Family Sharing

Once you have set up Family Sharing and added family members, you can start sharing a selection of items.

Sharing photos

Photos can be shared with Family Sharing thanks to the Family album that is created automatically within the Photos app. To use this:

Beware

iCloud Photo Sharing has to be turned On to enable Family Sharing (**Settings** > **Photos** > **iCloud Photo Sharing**).

Hot tip

When someone else in your Family Sharing circle adds a photo to the Family album, you are notified in the Notification Center and also by a red notification on the Photos app.

1. Tap once on the **Photos** app

2. Tap once on the **Shared** button

3. The **Family** album is already available in the **Shared** section. Tap once on the Cloud button to access the album and start adding photos to it

4. Tap once on this button to add photos to the album

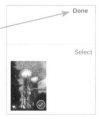

5. Tap on the photos you want to add, and tap once on the **Done** button

6. Make sure the **Family** album is selected as the Shared Album, and tap once on the **Post** button

Sharing calendars

Family Sharing also generates a Family calendar that can be used by all Family Sharing members:

1 Tap once on the **Calendar** app

2 Create a calendar event, as shown on pages 130-131, tap on the **Calendar** button and select the Family calendar to add the event to a calendar that all members of Family Sharing can see

Cancel	**New Event**	Add
All-day		⬤
Starts		Sat, Apr 14, 2018
Ends		Sat, Apr 14, 2018
Repeat		Never ›
Calendar		● Family ›

To change the color tag for a calendar, tap once on the Calendar button at the bottom-middle of the Calendar window. All of the current calendars will be shown. Tap once on the **i** symbol next to a calendar, and select a new color as required.

Sharing music, books and movies

Family Sharing means that all members of the group can share purchases from the iTunes Store, the App Store or the iBooks Store. To do this:

1 Open either the **iTunes Store**, **App Store** or **iBooks**

2 For the **App Store**, tap once on the Account icon and tap once on the **Purchased** button; or

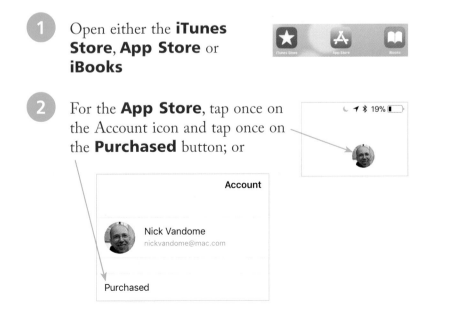

Account

Nick Vandome
nickvandome@mac.com

Purchased

...cont'd

for the **iTunes Store** and **iBooks**, tap once on the respective **Purchased** buttons on the bottom toolbar

3 For all three apps, tap once on a member under **Family Purchases** to view their purchases and download them, if required, by tapping once on this button

Don't forget

When the Find Friends app is opened, tap once on the **Add** button on the top toolbar to add family members. They also have to have Location Services turned **On** (**Settings** > **Privacy** > **Location Services**) so that you can locate them.

Finding family members

Family Sharing makes it easy to keep in touch with the rest of the family and see exactly where they are. This can be done with the Find Friends app. The other person must have their iPad (or other Apple device) turned on and be online. To find family members:

1 Tap once on the **Find Friends** app

2 The location of any people who are linked via your Family Sharing is displayed. Tap once on a person's name to view their location. Swipe outwards with thumb and forefinger to zoom in on the map

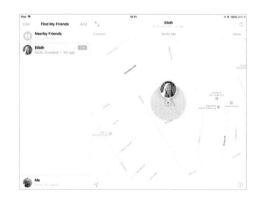

4 The iPad Keyboard

The iPad has a virtual keyboard and can also be used with an external one. This chapter shows how to manage the keyboard for entering content.

It's Virtually a Keyboard

The keyboard on the iPad is a virtual one; i.e. it appears on the touchscreen whenever text or numbered input is required for an app. This can be for a variety of reasons:

- Entering text with a word processing app, email or an organization app such as Notes.

- Entering a web address into a web browser such as the Safari app.

- Entering information into a form.

- Entering a password.

Viewing the keyboard

When you attempt one of the items above, the keyboard appears so that you can enter any text or numbers:

Around the keyboard

To access the various keyboard controls:

1 Tap once on the Shift button to create a **Cap** (capital) text letter

2 Double-tap on the Shift button to enable **Caps Lock**

3 Tap once on this button to back-delete an item

The keyboard has been redesigned in iOS 11.

In addition to the iPad virtual keyboard, it is also possible to use a traditional computer keyboard with the iPad. This can be particularly useful if you are using the iPad for a lot of typing. The keyboard is an Apple Wireless Keyboard, which connects via Bluetooth. This can be turned on in the Settings app, under the Bluetooth tab. The iPad Pro has a separate Apple Smart Keyboard (see page 13).

To return from Caps Lock, tap again on the Shift/Caps button.

Additional buttons

In previous versions of the iOS keyboard on the iPad there were separate keyboards for letters, numbers and symbols. However, in iOS 11 all items can be accessed from a single keyboard. To access numbers and symbols:

1 Swipe down on one of the keys on the top line of the keyboard to enter the equivalent number, rather than a letter

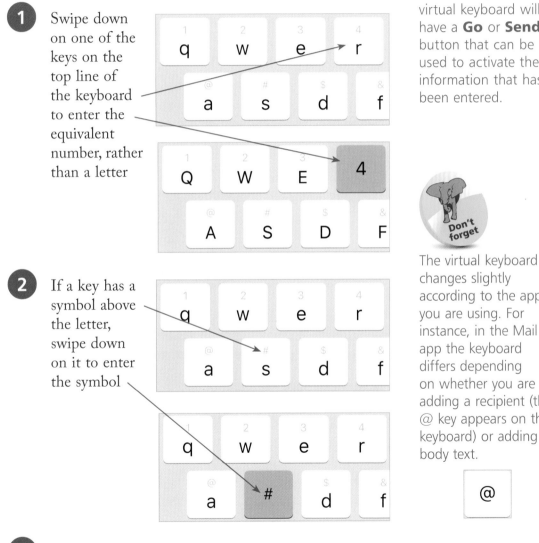

2 If a key has a symbol above the letter, swipe down on it to enter the symbol

3 Tap once on this button to hide the keyboard

71

Moving the Keyboard

By default, the keyboard appears as a single unit along the bottom of the screen. However, it is possible to undock the keyboard and also split it to appear on either side of the screen. To do this:

Hot tip

To redock the keyboard, press and hold on the button in Step 1 and tap once on the **Dock** button or, if the keyboard has been split, the **Dock and Merge** button.

Hot tip

The keyboard can also be split by swiping outwards on both sides, with one finger on each side. Reverse the process to merge it again.

1 Press and hold this button on the keyboard

2 Tap once on the **Undock** button

3 The keyboard is undocked from the bottom of the screen

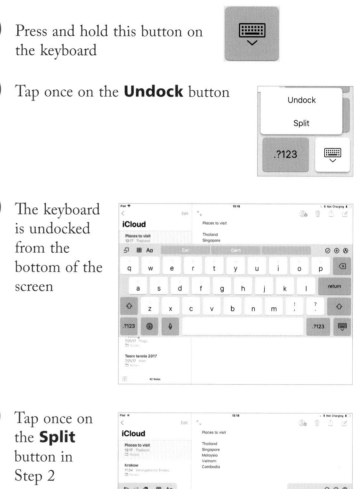

4 Tap once on the **Split** button in Step 2

5 The keyboard is split to the left and the right sides of the screen

Keyboard Settings

Settings for the keyboard can be determined in the General section of the Settings app. To do this:

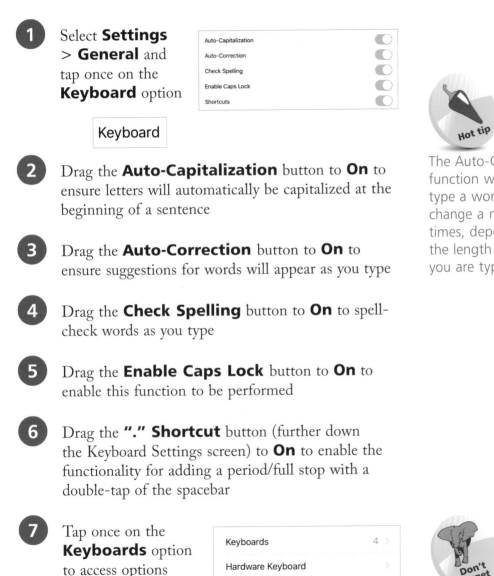

1 Select **Settings > General** and tap once on the **Keyboard** option

| Auto-Capitalization |
| Auto-Correction |
| Check Spelling |
| Enable Caps Lock |
| Shortcuts |

Keyboard

2 Drag the **Auto-Capitalization** button to **On** to ensure letters will automatically be capitalized at the beginning of a sentence

3 Drag the **Auto-Correction** button to **On** to ensure suggestions for words will appear as you type

4 Drag the **Check Spelling** button to **On** to spell-check words as you type

5 Drag the **Enable Caps Lock** button to **On** to enable this function to be performed

6 Drag the **"." Shortcut** button (further down the Keyboard Settings screen) to **On** to enable the functionality for adding a period/full stop with a double-tap of the spacebar

7 Tap once on the **Keyboards** option to access options for adding different keyboards

Keyboards	4 >
Hardware Keyboard	>
Text Replacement	>

8 Tap once on the **Text Replacement** option to view existing text shortcuts and also to create new ones

Hot tip

The Auto-Correction function works as you type a word, so it may change a number of times, depending on the length of the word you are typing.

73

Don't forget

For more information about Text Replacement, see page 79.

Entering Text

Once you have applied the keyboard settings that you require, you can start entering text. To do this:

 Tap once on the text entry area to activate the keyboard. Start typing with the keyboard. The text will appear at the point where you tapped on the screen

Don't forget

If Predictive text is On, the suggested word will appear above the keyboard on the QuickType bar (see page 76).

 If Predictive text is Off, as you type, Auto-Correction comes up with suggestions. Tap once on the spacebar to accept the suggestion, or tap once on the cross next to it to reject it

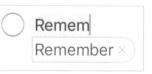

Don't forget

If you keep typing as normal, the Auto-Correction suggestion will disappear when you finish the word.

 Any misspelled words appear underlined in red

Remember to go to the supermrkt

 Tap once on this button to hide the keyboard

Editing Text

Once text has been entered it can be selected, copied, cut and pasted. Depending on the app being used, the text can also be formatted, such as with a word processing app.

Selecting text

To select text, and perform tasks on the text:

1 To change the insertion point, tap and hold until the magnifying glass appears

2 Drag the magnifying glass to move the insertion point

3 Tap once at the insertion point to access the menu buttons

4 Double-tap on a word to select it. Tap once on one of the menu buttons, as required

5 Drag the selection handles to expand or contract the selection

6 Use the Shortcuts bar on the keyboard to, from left to right, cut the selection, copy the selection, or paste an item

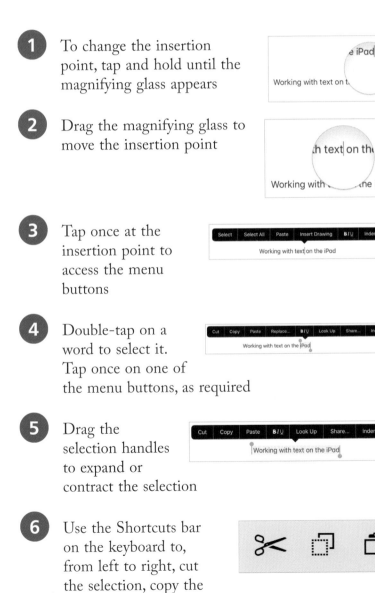

Hot tip

Once the menu buttons in Step 3 have been accessed, tap once on **Select** to select the previous word, or **Select All** to select all of the available text.

Hot tip

The menu buttons in Step 4 can be used to replace the selected word; add bold, italics or underlining to it; or view a definition of it (Look Up).

Hot tip

In some apps, the cursor can be moved by dragging anywhere on the screen with two fingers, including over the keyboard. Text can then be selected by single- or double-tapping.

Using Predictive Text

Predictive text tries to guess what you are typing, and also predicts the next word following the one you have just typed. It was developed primarily for text messaging, and it is included on the iPad with iOS 11. To use it:

1 Tap once on the **General** tab in the Settings app

2 Tap once on the **Keyboard** option

Keyboard	>

3 Drag the **Predictive** button **On**

Predictive	⬤

4 When Predictive text is activated, the QuickType bar is displayed above the keyboard. Initially, this has a suggestion for the first word to include. Tap on a word, or start typing

Don't forget

Predictive text learns from your writing style as you write, and so gets more accurate at predicting words.

5 As you type, suggestions appear. Tap on one to accept it. Tap on the word within the quotation marks to accept exactly what you have typed, or tap on another option

Hi, I was just beg

6 After you have typed a word, a suggestion for the next word appears. This can be selected by tapping on it, or ignored

Hi, I was just beginning

Hot tip

Third-party keyboards can be downloaded from the App Store and added to your iPad. Search "keyboard" in the App Store Search box. Keyboards that have been added (and also those for different languages) can be activated within **Settings** > **General** > **Keyboard** > **Keyboards** > **Add New Keyboard**. Press and hold on this button on the keyboard to switch between available keyboards.

77

Keyboard Shortcuts

There are two types of shortcuts that can be used on the iPad keyboard:

- Shortcuts using keys on the keyboard

- Shortcuts created with text abbreviations

Shortcuts with keys

The shortcuts that can be created with the keys on the keyboard are:

1 Double-tap on the spacebar to add a full stop/period and a space at the end of a sentence

Hot tip

The shortcut in Step 1 can be disabled by switching off the **"."** **Shortcut** option within the **Settings** > **General** > **Keyboard** section.

2 Swipe up once on the comma (or press and hold) to insert an apostrophe

3 Swipe up once on the full stop/period to insert quotation marks

4 Press and hold on appropriate letters to access accented versions for different languages

Text abbreviations

To create shortcuts with text abbreviations:

1 Tap once on the **Keyboard** option in the **General** section of the Settings app

Keyboard

2 Tap once on the **Text Replacement** option

Text Replacement

3 Tap once on this button to add a new shortcut ✛

4 Enter the phrase you want to be made into a shortcut

Phrase	My name is Nick

5 Enter the abbreviation you want to use as the shortcut for the phrase

Shortcut	mnn

6 Tap once on the **Save** button

Save

7 The shortcut is displayed here

11:18		⅍ Not Charging ▮
‹ Keyboards	**Text Replacement**	✛
M		A
mnn	My name is Nick	B C
O		D
omw	On my way	E F

8 Use the Search box or the alphabetical bar at the right-hand side to search for other shortcuts that have been created

Don't forget

The shortcut does not need to have the equivalent number of letters as words in the phrase. A 10-word phrase could have a two-letter shortcut.

Hot tip

To use a shortcut, enter the abbreviation. As you type, the phrase appears underneath the abbreviation. Tap once on the spacebar to add the phrase, or tap once on the cross to reject it. To delete a shortcut, in the Text Replacement section in Step 7 swipe on it from right to left and tap once on the **Delete** button.

Voice Typing

On the keyboard there is also a voice typing option, which enables you to enter text by speaking into a microphone, rather than typing on the keyboard. This is On by default.

Using voice typing

Voice typing can be used with any app with a text input function. To do this:

1 Tap once on this button on the keyboard to activate the voice typing microphone. Speak into the microphone to record text

2 As the voice typing function is processing the recording, this screen appears

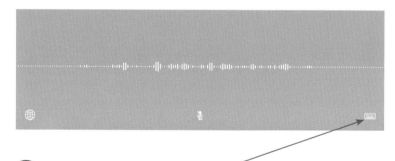

3 Tap once on the **Keyboard** button to finish recording and return to the virtual keyboard

4 Once the recording has been processed, the text appears in the app

Voice typing

Hello my name is Nick. This was done with my voice.

Beware

Voice typing is not an exact science, and you may find that some strange examples appear. The best results are created if you speak as clearly as possible and reasonably slowly.

Hot tip

The first time that you tap on the Microphone button you may be prompted to select the **Enable Dictation** button too. This can also be done within **Settings** > **General** > **Keyboard** > **Enable Dictation**.

Don't forget

There are other voice typing apps available from the App Store. Two to try are Dragon Anywhere and Voice Dictation.

5 Knowing your Apps

Apps keep the iPad engine running. This chapter details the built-in ones and shows how to obtain more through the App Store.

Don't forget

You need an active internet connection to download apps from the App Store.

Hot tip

Within a number of apps there is a **Share** button that can be used to share items through a variety of methods, including email, Facebook and Twitter. The Share button can also be used to share items using the AirDrop function over short distances with other compatible devices. To access these options, tap once on this button, where available.

What is an App?

An app is just a more modern name for a computer program. Initially, it was used in relation to mobile devices, such as the iPhone and the iPad, but it is now becoming more widely used with desktop and laptop computers, for both Mac and Windows operating systems.

On the iPad there are two types of apps:

- **Built-in apps**. These are the apps that come pre-installed on the iPad.

- **App Store apps**.
These are apps that can be downloaded from the online App Store. There is a huge range of apps available there, covering a variety of different categories. Some are free, while others have to be paid for. The apps in the App Store are updated and added to on a daily basis, so there are always new ones to explore.

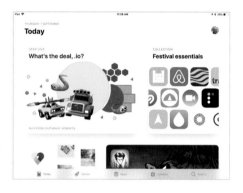

There are also two important points to remember about apps (both built-in and those from the App Store):

- Apart from some of the built-in apps, the majority of apps do not interact with each other. This means that there is less chance of viruses being transmitted from app to app on your iPad, and apps can also operate without a reliance on other apps.

- Content created by apps is saved within the app itself, rather than within a file structure on your iPad; e.g. if you create a note in the Notes app, it is saved there; if you take a photo, it is saved in the Photos app. Content is also usually saved automatically when it is created or edited, so you do not have to worry about saving as you work.

Built-in Apps

The built-in iPad apps are the ones that appear on the Home screen when you turn on the iPad:

The iPad **Settings** app is another of the built-in apps, and this is looked at in detail on pages 22-23.

- **App Store**. This can be used to access the App Store, from where additional apps can then be downloaded.

- **Calendar**. An app for storing appointments, important dates and other calendar information. It can be synced with iCloud.

- **Camera**. This gives direct access to the front-facing and rear-facing iPad cameras. You can also access your Photos gallery from here.

Some of the built-in apps, such as Mail and Contacts, interact with each other when required. However, since these are designed by Apple, there is little chance of them containing viruses.

- **Clock**. This displays the current time and can be used to view the time in different countries, and also as an alarm clock and a stopwatch.

- **Contacts**. An address book app. Once contacts are added here they can then also be accessed from other apps, such as Mail.

- **FaceTime**. This is an app that uses the built-in front-facing camera on the iPad to hold video chats with other iPad users, or those with an iPhone, iPod Touch or a Mac computer.

...cont'd

The Files app is a new feature in iOS 11.

There have to be compatible devices in the home in order for the Home app to work with them.

You need an Apple ID to obtain iBooks. They are downloaded in a matter of seconds, and you cannot change your mind once you have entered your Apple ID details. For full details about obtaining an Apple ID, see page 99.

● **Files**. This is a new app in iOS 11 that can be used to display and access files held on your iPad, in the iCloud Drive and other online file storage services, such as Dropbox.

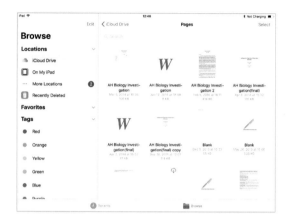

● **Find Friends**. This is an app that can be used to view the location of anyone who is part of your Family Sharing group in iCloud.

● **Find iPhone**. This is an app that can be used to locate any other of your Apple devices, or those of Family Sharing members.

● **Home**. This can be used to control certain compatible functions within the home, such as heating controls.

● **iBooks**. This is an app for downloading electronic books, which can then be read on the iPad. This can be done for both plain text and illustrated iBooks.

● **iTunes Store**. This app can be used to browse the iTunes store, where music, TV shows, movies, and more can be downloaded to your iPad.

● **Mail**. This is the email app for sending and receiving email on your iPad.

- **Maps**. Use this app to view maps from around the world, find specific locations and get directions to destinations.

- **Messages**. This is the iPad messaging service, which can be used between iPads, iPhones, iPod Touches and Mac computers. It can be used with not only text, but also photos and videos.

- **Music**. An app for playing music on your iPad and also accessing the Apple Music service, which connects to the whole iTunes library.

- **News**. This is an app that collates news stories and content from numerous sources.

- **Notes**. If you need to jot down your thoughts or ideas, this app is perfect for just that.

- **Photo Booth**. This is an app for creating fun and creative effects with your photos.

- **Photos**. This is an app for viewing and editing photos, creating slideshows, and for viewing the videos you have taken with your iPad camera. It can also be used to share photos via iCloud.

- **Podcasts**. This can be used to download and play podcasts from within the App Store.

- **Reminders**. Use this app for organization, when you want to create to-do lists and set reminders for events.

- **Safari**. The Apple web browser that has been developed for viewing the web on your iPad.

- **Tips**. This can be used to display tips and hints for items on your iPad.

- **Videos**. This is an app for viewing videos purchased from the iTunes Store on your iPad, and also streaming them to a larger HDTV monitor.

Hot tip

It is worth investing in a good pair of headphones for listening to music so you do not disturb other people.

Don't forget

A podcast is an audio and sometimes video program, and they cover an extensive range of subjects.

Don't forget

The Tips and Podcasts apps are sometimes grouped together in a folder named Extras (see pages 94-95 for more information on working with folders).

85

About the App Store

While the built-in apps that come with the iPad are flexible and versatile, it really comes into its own when you connect to the App Store. This is an online resource containing thousands of apps that can be downloaded and then used on your iPad, including categories from Lifestyle to Travel.

To use the App Store, you must first have an Apple ID. This can be obtained when you first connect to the App Store. Once you have an Apple ID you can start exploring the App Store:

Don't forget

For full details about obtaining an Apple ID, see page 99.

The App Store has been enhanced in iOS 11.

The dedicated Games section is a new feature in iOS 11.

 Tap once on the **App Store** app on the Home screen

 The App Store Home screen (**Today**) displays the latest current recommended apps, on a daily basis. Swipe up the page to move to other daily recommendations, including the Daily List

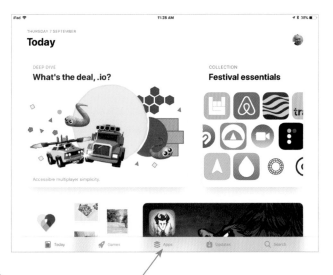

 Tap on the buttons on the bottom toolbar to view the apps according to **Today**, **Games**, **Apps** and **Updates**

Viewing apps

To view apps in the App Store and read about their content and functionality:

 Tap once on an app

 General details about the app are displayed

 Swipe up the page to view reviews about the app

If it is an upgraded version of an app, this page will include details of any fixes and improvements that have been made.

4 Swipe up the page to view more information about the app

5 Tap once on the **Get** button to download a free app about the app (a paid-for one will display a price)

Finding Apps

Within the App Store, apps are separated into categories according to type. This enables you to find apps according to particular subjects. To do this:

1 Tap once on the **Apps** button on the bottom toolbar

2 Details of the latest apps are displayed

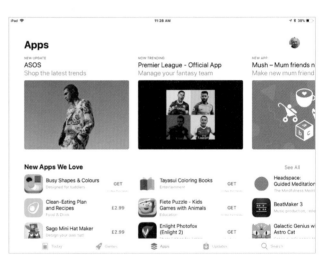

88

3 Scroll down the page (by swiping up) to view the different sections. Tap once on the **See All** button to view all of the items in a section

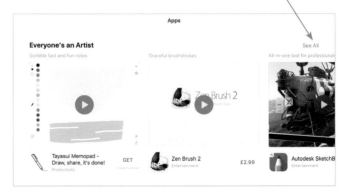

...cont'd

Categories

To view the different categories in the App Store:

1 Tap once on the **Apps** button on the bottom toolbar

Apps

2 Swipe up the page to the **Top Categories** section

Top Categories   See All

🛍 Entertainment   🎓 Education

✏ Productivity   📷 Photo & Video

🔢 Utilities   ♪♫ Music

3 Tap once on the **See All** button to view all of the available categories

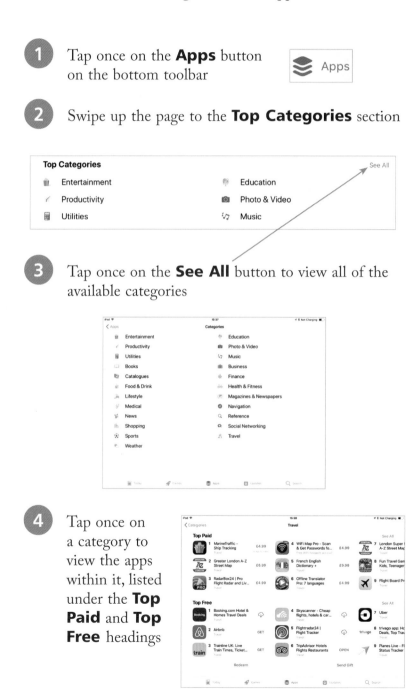

4 Tap once on a category to view the apps within it, listed under the **Top Paid** and **Top Free** headings

...cont'd

Top Charts

To find the top-rated apps:

1 Tap once on the **Apps** button on the bottom toolbar

2 Swipe up the page to view the current **Top Paid** and **Top Free** apps

3 Tap once on the **See All** button to see the full range of paid for and free apps

4 Tap once on the **All Categories** button, and tap once on a category to view the Top Paid and Top Free apps for that category

Beware

Do not limit yourself to just viewing the top apps. Although these are the most popular, there are also a lot of excellent apps within each category.

...cont'd

Searching for apps

Another way to find apps is with the App Store Search box, which is located at the right of the bottom toolbar of the App Store. To use this:

1 Tap once on the **Search** button on the bottom toolbar, and tap once in the **Search** box to bring up the iPad virtual keyboard

For more information about using the iPad virtual keyboard, see Chapter 4.

2 Enter a search keyword or phrase. Suggestions appear as you are typing

3 Tap once on a result to view the related app and information about it

Obtaining and Updating Apps

When you identify an app that you would like to use, it can be downloaded to your iPad. To do this:

Don't forget

Apps usually download in a few minutes or less, depending on the speed of your internet connection.

Beware

Some apps have "in-app purchases". This is additional content that has to be paid for when it is downloaded.

1 Find the app you want to download, and tap once on the button next to the app (this will say **Get** or will have a price)

Stop, Breathe & Think
Meditation tuned to your feels
GET
4.5 ★★★★☆

2 Tap once on the **Enter Password** button

Enter Password

3 Enter your Apple ID details here

Sign In with Apple ID

Enter the password for Apple ID "nickvandome@mac.com" to get Stop,...

●●●●●●●●

4 The app will begin to download onto your iPad

Loading...

5 Once the app is downloaded, tap on it to open and use it

Spanish
Spending
TripAdvisor
Breathe

Updating apps

The world of apps is a dynamic and fast-moving one, and new apps are being created and added to the App Store on a daily basis. Existing apps are also being updated, to improve their performance, security and functionality. Once you have installed an app from the App Store, it is possible to obtain updates at no extra cost (whether or not the app was paid for). To do this:

1 When an update is available it is denoted by a red numbered icon on the App Store app, showing how many updates are available

2 Tap once on the **App Store** app

3 In the App Store, tap on the **Updates** button, located on the bottom toolbar

4 The available updates are displayed

5 Tap on the button next to an app to update it

6 Tap on the **Update All** button in the top-right corner to update all of the required apps

Update All

You should keep your apps as up-to-date as possible to take advantage of software fixes and updates.

The notification labels on apps (such as the App Store and the Mail app) can be turned On or Off in **Settings** > **Notifications** > **[select app]** > drag **Badge App Icon** to **On** or **Off**.

It is possible to set updates to apps to download automatically: **Settings** > **iTunes & App Store** > **Automatic Downloads**. Drag the buttons to **On** for the required items.

93

Organizing Apps

When you start downloading apps you will probably soon find that you have dozens, if not hundreds, of them. You can move between screens to view all of your apps by swiping left or right with one finger.

Hot tip

To move an app between screens, press and hold on it until it starts to jiggle and a cross appears in the corner. Then drag it to the side of the screen. If there is space on the next screen, the app will be moved there.

As more apps are added it can become hard to find the apps you want, particularly if you have to swipe between several screens. However, it is possible to organize apps into individual folders to make using them more manageable. To do this:

 Press on an app until it starts to jiggle and a cross appears at the top-left corner

 Drag the app over another one

3 A folder is created, containing the two apps

Beware

Only top-level folders can be created; i.e. sub-folders cannot be created. Also, one folder cannot be placed within another.

4 The folder is given a default name, usually based on the category of the apps

5 Tap on the folder name, and type a new name if required

6 Click the **Home** button once to finish creating the folder

Hot tip

If you want to rename an apps folder after it has been created, press and hold on it until it starts to jiggle. Then tap on it once and edit the name, as in Step 5.

7 Click the **Home** button again to return to the Home screen (this is done whenever you want to return to the Home screen from an apps folder)

8 The folder is added on the Home screen. Tap once on this to access the items within it

Deleting Apps

If you decide that you do not want certain apps anymore, they can be deleted from your iPad. However, they remain in the iCloud so that you can reinstall them if you change your mind. This also means that if you delete an app by mistake, you can get it back from the App Store without having to pay for it again. To delete an app:

96

 Press on an app until it starts to jiggle and a cross appears at the top-left corner

iTunes U

 Tap once on the cross to delete the app. In the Delete dialog box, tap once on the **Delete** button. The app is then uninstalled from your iPad

Delete "iTunes U"?
Deleting this app will also delete its data.

Cancel   Delete

To reinstall an app:

 Tap once on the **App Store** app

App Store

 Tap once on the **Search** button on the bottom toolbar

Q Search

 Enter the name of the app in the Search box, and tap once on the **iCloud** icon to download it again

Filters ⌄   Q itunes u

iTunes U
Free educational courses
★★★☆☆

6 Keeping in Touch

This chapter shows how to use your iPad to keep ahead in the fast-moving world of online communications, using email, social media, video calls and a range of texting options.

Getting Online

iPads can be used for a variety of different communications, but they all require online access. This is done via Wi-Fi, and you will need to have an Internet Service Provider and a Wi-Fi router to connect to the internet. Once this is in place, you will be able to connect to a Wi-Fi network.

Don't forget

If you have the 4G/3G version of the iPad you can obtain internet access this way, but this has to be done through a provider of this service, as with a cell/mobile phone.

1 Tap once on the **Settings** app

2 Tap once on the **Wi-Fi** tab

🛜 Wi-Fi   Off

3 Ensure the **Wi-Fi** button is in the **On** position

Wi-Fi ⬤

4 Available networks are shown here. Tap once on yours to select it

CHOOSE A NETWORK...
PlusnetWireless792287
VM997653-5G
Other...

Don't forget

If you are connecting to your home Wi-Fi network, the iPad should connect automatically each time, once it has been set up. If you are connecting in a public Wi-Fi area, you will be asked which network you would like to join.

5 Enter the password for your Wi-Fi router

Enter the password for "PlusnetWireless792287"

Cancel   **Enter Password**   Join

Password ●●●●●●●●●|

6 Tap once on the **Join** button

Join

7 Once a network has been joined, a tick appears next to it. This now provides access to the internet

Wi-Fi ⬤

✓ PlusnetWireless792287   🔒 🛜 ⓘ

Obtaining an Apple ID

An Apple ID is an email address and password registered with Apple that enables you to log in and use a variety of online Apple services. These include:

- App Store

- iTunes Store and Apple Music

- iCloud

- Messages

- FaceTime

- iBooks

It is free to register for an Apple ID, and this can be done when you access one of the apps or services which require it, or, you can register on the Apple website at Apple ID (**https://appleid.apple.com**):

If you are using an Apple ID to buy items such as from iTunes or the App Store, you will need to provide a valid method of payment.

 Tap once on the **Create Your Apple ID** button at the top of the Apple ID web page

> Create Your Apple ID

 Enter the details for the **Create Your Apple ID** wizard to set up your Apple ID account

Settings > **Apple ID** is where you can access your Apple ID details and edit them, if required.

Create Your Apple ID

One Apple ID is all you need to access all Apple services.
Already have an Apple ID? Find it here >

first name | last name

United States

birthday

name@example.com
This will be your new Apple ID.

password

confirm password

Setting up an Email Account

Email accounts

Email settings can be specified within the Settings app. Different email accounts can also be added. To do this:

Hot tip

If you don't already have an email account set up, you can choose one of the providers from the list and you will be guided through the setup process. You may also find our title, **Internet for Seniors in easy steps** useful. Visit our online shop at www.ineasysteps.com

100

Hot tip

If your email provider is not on the **Add Account** list, tap once on **Other** at the bottom of the list and complete the account details using the information from your email provider.

1 Tap once on the **Settings** app

2 Tap once on the **Accounts & Passwords** tab

3 Tap once on the **Add Account** option to add a new account

4 Tap once on the type of email account you want to add

5 Enter your login details for the account. Follow the wizard for the account, and tap on the **Next** button at each stage

6 Drag these buttons **On** or **Off** to specify which functions are to be available for the required account

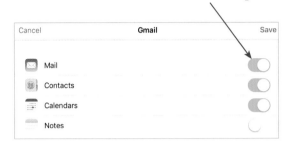

If you set up more than one email account, messages from all of them can be downloaded and displayed by **Mail**.

7 Each new account is added under the **Accounts** heading of the Accounts & Passwords section

Email settings

Email settings can be specified within the Settings app. Different email accounts can also be added there.

1 Under the **Mail** section, there are several options for how Mail operates and looks. These include the number of lines for previewing an email in the Inbox, options for managing emails by swiping on them, and options for flagging emails

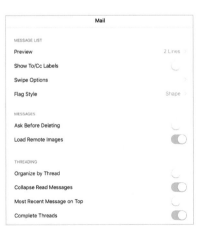

The **Organize by Thread** option can be turned **On** to show connected email conversations within your Inbox. If there is a thread of emails, this is indicated by this symbol:

Tap on it once to view the thread.

Emailing

Email on the iPad is created, sent and received using the Mail app. This provides a range of functionality for managing email, including adding mailboxes and viewing email conversation threads.

Accessing Mail

To access Mail, and start sending and receiving emails:

Hot tip

To quickly delete an email from your Inbox, swipe on it from right to left and tap once on the **Trash** (Delete) button. This also generates options to **Flag** the email and a **More** button, from which you can reply, forward, mark or move the current email.

 Tap once on the **Mail** app (the red icon in the corner displays the number of unread emails in your Inbox)

 Tap once on a message to display it in the main panel

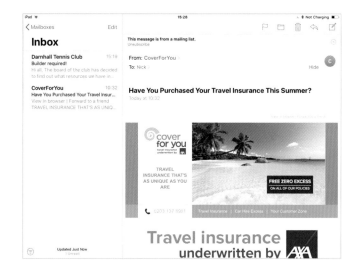

Don't forget

If the **Fetch New Data** option (**Settings** > **Accounts & Password** > **Fetch New Data**) is set to **Push**, new emails will be downloaded automatically from your mail server. To check manually for new downloads, swipe down from the top of the mailbox pane.

 Use these buttons to, from left to right, flag a message, move a message, delete a message, respond to a message and create a new message

4 Tap once on this button to reply to a message, forward it to a new recipient, or print it

Reply
Forward
Print

Creating email

To create and send an email:

1 Tap once on this button to create a new message

2 In the **To** box, enter the recipient's email address, or type the recipient's name (if they are in your Contacts app), and tap on one of the suggestions to select it

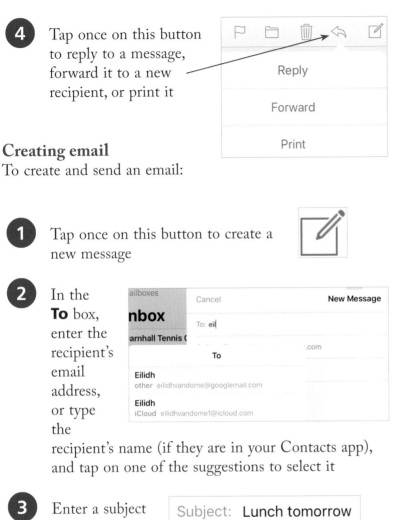

3 Enter a subject

Subject: **Lunch tomorrow**

4 Enter the body text

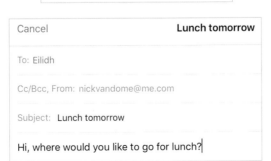

Cancel   **Lunch tomorrow**

To: Eilidh

Cc/Bcc, From: nickvandome@me.com

Subject: Lunch tomorrow

Hi, where would you like to go for lunch?

5 Tap once on the **Send** button to send the email to the recipient

Hot tip

If the recipient has been added to your Contacts app (see page 132), their details will appear as you type. Tap once on the email address, if it appears, to include it in the **To** box.

103

...cont'd

Mailboxes

Different categories of email messages can be managed via Mailboxes. For instance, you may want to keep your social emails separate from ones that apply to financial activities.

1. From your Inbox, tap once on the **Mailboxes** button

Mailboxes
Edit
Inbox
Search

2. The current mailboxes are displayed. Tap once on the **Edit** button

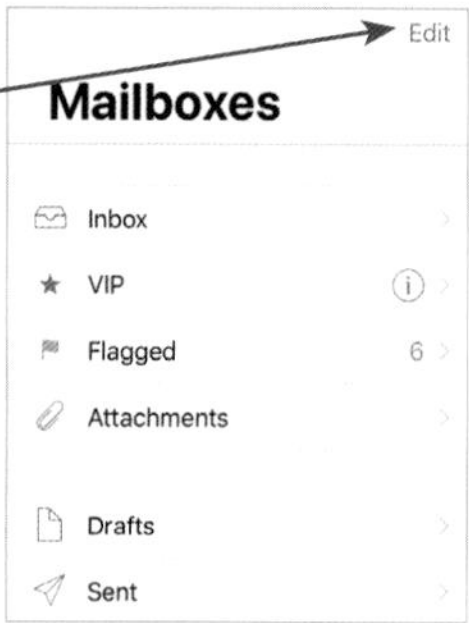
Edit
Mailboxes
Inbox
VIP
Flagged
6
Attachments
Drafts
Sent

3. Tap once on the **New Mailbox** button at the bottom of the Mailboxes panel

New Mailbox

4. Enter a name for the new mailbox. Tap once on the **Save** button

Cancel
New Mailbox
Save
iPad
MAILBOX LOCATION
iCloud

5. Tap once on the **Done** button

Done

6. To delete a mailbox, tap on it from the Edit window accessed in Step 2. In the subsequent **Edit Mailbox** window, tap on the **Delete Mailbox** button

Cancel
Edit Mailbox
Save
iPad
MAILBOX LOCATION
iCloud
Delete Mailbox

Hot tip

Messages can be edited within individual mailboxes. To do this, select a mailbox and tap once on the **Edit** button. The message can then be edited with the **Mark**, **Move** or **Trash/Delete** options at the bottom of the window.

Don't forget

One mailbox that can be included is for VIPs, i.e. your most important contacts. To add these from an email, tap and hold on the person's name in an email you receive from them, then tap once on the **Add to VIP** button. Under **Mailboxes**, tap once on **VIP** to view emails from all of your VIPs.

Adding Social Media

Using social media sites such as Facebook, Twitter and Snapchat to keep in touch with family and friends has now become common across all generations. On the iPad with iOS 11, it is possible to download a range of social media apps and also view updates through the Notification Center (see second tip). To add social media apps:

Social media websites can also be accessed directly through the Safari web browser.

1 Open the App Store and navigate to the **Apps** > **Categories** > **Social Networking** section

Social Networking

2 Tap once on the required apps to download them to your iPad

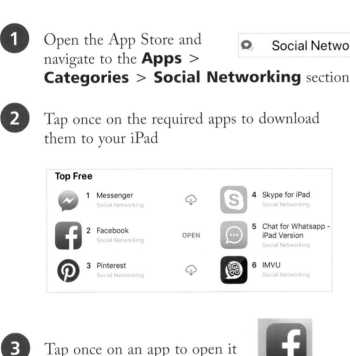

Top Free

1 Messenger
Social Networking

2 Facebook
Social Networking — OPEN

3 Pinterest
Social Networking

4 Skype for iPad
Social Networking

5 Chat for Whatsapp - iPad Version
Social Networking

6 IMVU
Social Networking

3 Tap once on an app to open it

Facebook

4 If you already have an account with the social media service, enter your login details, or tap once on the **Sign Up** button to create a new account

Email or phone number

Password

Log In

Sign Up for Facebook   Need Help?

Social media updates for some apps can be set to appear in your **Notification Center**. Open **Settings** and tap once on the **Notifications** tab. Under the **Notification Style** heading, tap once on the social networking site and select options for how you would like the notifications to appear.

105

Text Messaging

Text messaging should not be thought of as the domain of the younger generation. On your iPad you can join the world of text with the Apple iMessage service that is accessed via the Messages app. This enables text, photo, video, emojis and audio messages to be sent, free of charge, between users of iOS on the iPad, iPhone, iPod Touch and Mac computers. iMessages can be sent to cell/mobile phone numbers and email addresses. To use Messages:

Don't forget

You need an Apple ID to send iMessages.

Don't forget

iMessages are sent using Wi-Fi. If a Wi-Fi connection is not available the message cannot be sent, unless the iPad has a cellular network connection.

Don't forget

If an iPad has a cellular network connection then this can be used to send regular text messages to other compatible devices such as cell/mobile phones. If the recipient is not using iMessages, the message will be sent as a standard SMS (Short Message Service). By default, iMessages appear in blue bubbles and SMS messages in green bubbles.

 Tap once on the **Messages** app

 Tap once on this button to create a new message and start a new conversation

 Tap once on this button to select someone from your contacts

4 Tap once on a contact to select them as the recipient of the new message

Groups	**Contacts**	Cancel
	Q Search	
E		
Paul **Eddy**		A
Eilidh		D

5 Tap once in the text box, and type with the keyboard to create a message. Tap once on this button to send the message

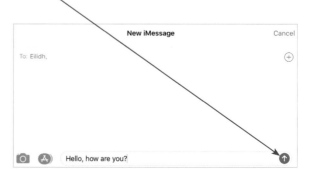

6 As the conversation progresses, each message is displayed in the main window

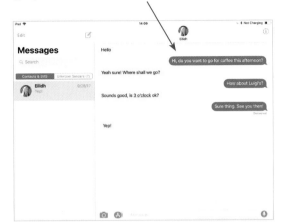

Hot tip

Press and hold on a message, and tap on the **More...** button that appears. Select a message, or messages, and tap on the **Trash** icon to remove them.

7 To edit whole conversations, tap once on the **Edit** button in the Messages panel

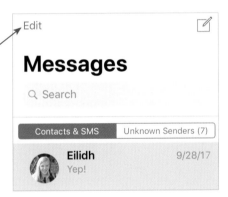

Edit

8 Tap once here to select the conversation, and tap once on the **Delete** button at the bottom of the page to delete the conversation

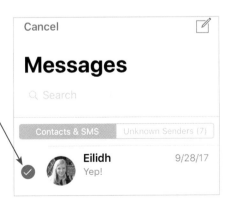

Delete

Don't forget

When a message has been sent, you are notified underneath it when it has been delivered.

Enhancing Text Messages

Adding emojis

Emojis (small graphical symbols) are becoming more common in text messages, and there is now a huge range that can be included with iOS 11. To use these:

1 Tap once on this button on the keyboard to view the emoji keyboards

2 Swipe left and right to view the emoji options. Tap once on an emoji to add it to a message

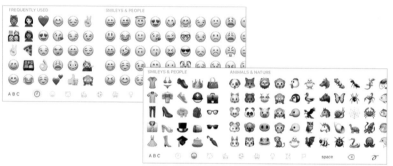

Don't forget

Emojis can be added automatically to replace certain words. Add text, and tap once on the Emoji button in the first Step 1. Any items that can be replaced by an emoji are highlighted. Tap once on the highlighted word to add the emoji.

Bubble effects

iMessages can also be sent with certain animated effects:

1 Write a message and press on this button

2 Tap once on the **Bubble** button at the top of the window, and tap once on one of the options. These are **Slam**, which creates a message that moves in at speed from the side of the screen; **Loud**, which creates a message in large text; **Gentle**, which creates a message in small text; and **Invisible Ink**, which creates a message that is concealed and then reveals the text

Don't forget

If Predictive text is turned **On**, emoji suggestions will appear in the QuickType bar above the keyboard (see pages 76-77).

Screen effects

iMessages can also be sent with full-screen effects:

1 Repeat Step 1 for Bubble effects on the previous page and tap once on the **Screen** button at the top of the window. Swipe left and right to view the full-screen effects

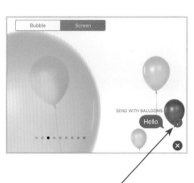

2 Tap once on this button to send the message

Quick replies (also known as Tapback)

It is possible to add a quick reply, in icon format. To do this:

1 Press and hold on the message to which you want to add a quick reply,

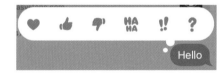

and tap once on one of the icons. This is sent to the recipient, attached to the original message

Adding stickers

Stickers and graphics can also be added to messages:

1 Tap once on this button next to the text box

2 Tap once on the **Visit Store** button to download sticker sets from the App Store, which can be added from the button in Step 1 above

---

Some messages, such as "Happy Birthday" and "Congratulations" automatically create full-screen effects.

You can turn off the full-screen effects – go to **Settings** > **General** > **Accessibility** and enable **Reduce Motion**.

Handwritten messages can also be created. Tap once on this button on the keyboard to access the handwriting panel. Write using your finger or an Apple Pencil (with the iPad Pro) and tap once on the **Done** button to add it to a message. The text appears animated to the recipient.

Having a Video Chat

Video chatting is a very personal and interactive way to keep in touch with family and friends around the world. The FaceTime app provides this facility with other iPad, iPhone and iPod Touch users, or a Mac computer with FaceTime. To use FaceTime for video chatting:

Don't forget

To make video calls with FaceTime you need an active internet connection and to be signed in with your Apple ID.

1 Tap once on the **FaceTime** app

2 Recent video chats are shown under the Video tab. Tap once here to select a contact

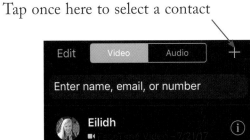

Hot tip

The contacts for FaceTime calls are taken from the iPad Contacts app (see page 132). You can also add new contacts directly to the contacts list by tapping once on the **+** icon and adding the relevant details for the new contact.

3 Tap once on a contact to access their details for making a FaceTime call

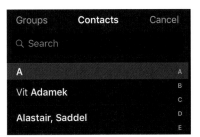

Don't forget

Skype is another option for making free video calls to other Skype users. The app can be downloaded from the App Store.

4 Tap once on the FaceTime video buttons to make a FaceTime call. The recipient must have FaceTime on their iPad, iPhone, iPod Touch or Mac computer

5 Once you have selected a contact, FaceTime starts connecting with them and displays this at the top of the screen

6 When you have connected, your contact appears in the main window and you appear in a picture-in-picture thumbnail in the corner

Don't forget

It is possible to silence incoming FaceTime calls and other alerts, at times when you do not want to be disturbed. This is done within **Do Not Disturb** in the **Settings** app. Drag the **Scheduled** button to **On** to specify times during which you do not want to be disturbed. If required, calls from selected people can still be enabled via the **Allow Calls From** option, under the **Phone** heading.

111

7 Tap once on this button to take a Live Photo of the screen (this is a photo that is created as a small animation). Both devices require iOS 11 for this

8 Tap once on this button to end the FaceTime call

NEW

Live Photos in FaceTime is a new feature in iOS 11 on the iPad.

9 If someone else makes a call to you, tap once on the **Decline** or **Accept** buttons

On Facebook you can have private text conversations with your friends, as well as posting public information for all of your friends to see. For more information, check out **Facebook for Beginners in easy steps** in our online shop at www. ineasysteps.com

Beware

When you follow people on Twitter, their Tweets appear on your Homepage feed. If they are very prolific, or you follow a lot of people, this may result in a lot of messages to read.

Communication Apps

Within the App Store there is a range of communication apps that can be used to contact friends and family via text, phone and video. There are also several apps for sharing information, updates and photos. Some of these are:

- **Facebook**. The social networking phenomenon that has over a billion users around the world. This app enables you to create and use a Facebook account from your iPad. You can then interact with friends and family by posting messages, comments and photos.

- **Twitter**. Another one of the top social networking sites on the web. It provides the facility to post text or news messages (Tweets) of up to 140 characters. You can choose other users to follow, so you see their Tweets, and other people can follow you to see yours, too.

- **Snapchat**. This is a popular photo and video sharing app: items can be shared for a limited period of time and they are then deleted. (The app is listed as iPhone only in the App Store but can be downloaded and used on the iPad: select **Filters** > **Supports** > **iPhone Only** in the App Store when searching for it).

- **Flickr**. An iPad version of the popular photo and video sharing site. You have to register for an account, and once you have done this you can share your photos and videos with a vast online community.

- **Skype**. The widely-used service for making video and voice calls. This is free when both users are using Skype over Wi-Fi. Skype can also be used for text messaging.

- **WordPress**. A web publishing app that can be used to create online blogs and your own websites.

- **Gmail**. If you have a Gmail account this will enable you to access it directly from your iPad.

- **myMail**. This can be used to access email from Hotmail/ Outlook, Gmail and Yahoo Mail accounts.

7 On a Web Safari

This chapter shows how to use the functionality of the built-in iPad web browser, Safari, to access the web and start enjoying the benefits of the online world.

Around Safari

The Safari app is the default web browser on the iPad. This can be used to view web pages, save favorites and read pages with the Reader function. To start using Safari:

When you tap in the Address Bar you also have the option of opening a page by tapping on one of the icons which appear in the Favorites window, below the Address Bar. See page 118 for more details about this.

As you type in the Address Bar, the options and suggestions below it become more defined.

Other browsers can be downloaded from the App Store. Some to try are: Chrome; My Web Browser; Dolphin Web Browser; Flash Browser; Firefox web browser and Opera Mini web browser.

 1 Tap once on the **Safari** app

 2 Tap once on the Address Bar at the top of the Safari window. Type a web page address

3 Tap once on the **Go** button on the keyboard to open the web page, or select one of the options below the Address Bar

4 The selected page opens with the top toolbar visible. As you scroll down the page, this disappears to give you a greater viewing area. Tap on the top of the screen, or scroll back up to display the toolbar again

5 Swipe up and down and left and right to navigate around the page

When a page opens in Safari, a blue status bar underneath the Address Bar indicates the progress of the loading page.

6 Swipe outwards with thumb and forefinger to zoom in on a web page (pinch inwards to zoom back out)

Double-tap with one finger to zoom in on a page by a set amount. Double-tap again with one finger to return to normal view. If the page has been zoomed by a greater amount by pinching, double-tap with two fingers to return to normal view.

Safari Settings

Settings for Safari can be specified in the Settings app.

Beware

If other people have access to the iPad, don't use **AutoFill** for names and passwords for any sites with sensitive information, such as banking sites.

Hot tip

If the **Open New Tabs in Background** is set to **On**, you can press and hold a link on a web page and select **Open in New Tab**. The link then opens in a new tab behind the one you are viewing.

Don't forget

Cookies are small items from websites that obtain details from your browser when you visit a site. The cookie remembers the details for the next time you visit the site.

1 Open the Settings app and tap once on the **Safari** tab

2 Tap once on the **Search Engine** link to select a default search engine to use

Search Engine

3 Tap once here for options for filling in online forms

GENERAL

AutoFill

4 Drag this button to **On** to open new pages in the background of your current page

Open New Tabs in Background

5 Drag this button to **On** to keep the Favorites Bar in view under the Address Bar in Safari

Show Favorites Bar

6 Tap once on the **Block All Cookies** link to specify how Safari deals with cookies from websites

Block All Cookies

7 Tap once on **Clear History and Website Data** to remove these

Clear History and Website Data

8 Drag this button to **On** to enable alerts for when you visit a fraudulent website

Fraudulent Website Warning

9 Drag this button to **On** to block pop-up messages

Block Pop-ups

Navigating Pages

When you are viewing pages within Safari there are a number of functions that can be used:

1 Tap once on these arrows to move forward and back between web pages that have been visited

2 Tap once here to view bookmarked pages, Reading List pages and browsing History (see page 121)

3 Tap once here to add a bookmark (see page 120); add to a Reading List; add an icon to your iPad Home screen; email a link to a page; share using social media, messaging and other apps; or print a page

4 Tap once here to open a new tab (see page 118)

5 Tap and hold a link to access additional options including: Open the link, Open in New Tab, Open in Split View, Add to Reading List, Copy or Share using a selection of options

6 Tap and hold on an image, and tap once on **Save Image** or **Copy**

Save Image
Copy

Tap and hold on the **Forward** and **Back** arrows in Step 1 to view lists of previously-visited pages in these directions. See page 120 for more on bookmarking.

If a web page has the button below in the Address Bar/Search box, it means that the page can be viewed with the **Reader** function. This displays the page as text and limited images, without any of the accompanying design to distract from the content. Tap on the button so that it turns black to activate the Reader.

The items that appear in the Favorites window can be determined within **Settings** > **Safari** and tapping once on the **Favorites** option.

Press and hold on this button to access options for opening Split View (see page 36 for details), opening a new tab, opening a new private tab, or closing all of the currently open tabs.

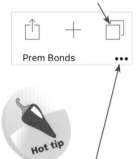

If there are too many items to be displayed on the Favorites Bar, tap once on this button to view the other items.

Opening New Tabs

Safari supports tabbed browsing, which means that you can open separate pages within the same window and access them by tapping on each tab at the top of the page:

1 Tap once here to open a new tab for another page

2 Open a new page by entering a web address into the Address Bar, or tap on one of the thumbnails in the **Favorites** window

3 Tap once on the tab headings to move between tabbed pages

4 Tap once on the cross to the top-left of a tab to close the active tab

Tab View

Tabs can be managed using iOS 11 on the iPad so that you can view all of your open Safari tabs on one screen, including those on other compatible Apple devices. To do this:

1 Tap once here to activate Tab View

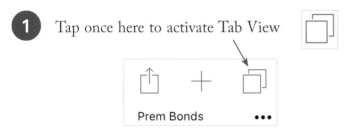

2 All of the currently-open tabs are displayed. Tap on one to open it

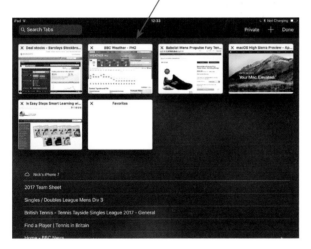

3 If you have open Safari tabs on other Apple devices, these will be shown at the bottom of the window

4 Tap once on this button at the top of the window to open another tab

5 Tap once on this button to open a **Private** tab, where no browsing history will be recorded during this browsing session

Hot tip

Tab View can also be activated by pinching inwards with thumb and forefinger on a web page that is at normal magnification, i.e. 1 to 1.

Don't forget

Tap once on the **Done** button at the top of the Tab View window to exit this, and return to the web page that was being viewed when Tab View was activated.

Bookmarking Pages

Once you start using Safari you will soon build up a collection of favorite pages that you visit regularly. To access these quickly, they can be bookmarked so that you can go to them in one tap. To set up and use bookmarks:

1 Open a web page that you want to bookmark. Tap once here to access the sharing options

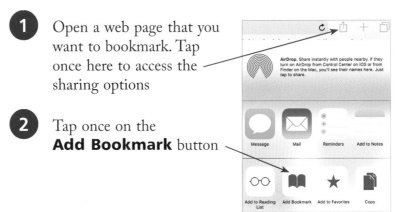

2 Tap once on the **Add Bookmark** button

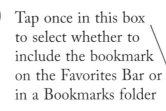

Don't forget

The Favorites Bar appears underneath the Address Bar in Safari. This includes items that have been added as bookmarks.

3 Tap once in this box to select whether to include the bookmark on the Favorites Bar or in a Bookmarks folder

4 Tap once on the **Save** button

Hot tip

For pages that you access frequently, you can also choose to **Add to Home Screen** from the sharing options in Step 2 (swipe from right to left on the bottom icons to access this option).

5 On the web page, tap once here to view all of the bookmarks. The Bookmarks folders are listed. Tap once on the **Edit** button at the bottom of the panel to delete or rename the folders

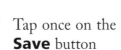

Reading List and History

The button in Step 5 on the previous page can also be used to access your Reading List and History.

Reading List

This is a list of web pages that have been saved for reading at a later date. The great thing about this function is that the pages can be read even when you are offline and not connected to the internet.

 1   Tap on this button to view your **Reading List**

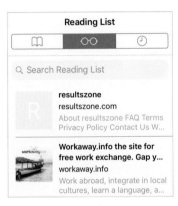

Reading List items can be added from the **Share** button in Step 1 on the previous page.

History

The History button displays your Safari browsing history.

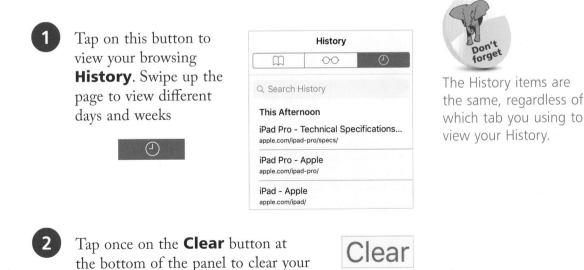

1   Tap on this button to view your browsing **History**. Swipe up the page to view different days and weeks

The History items are the same, regardless of which tab you using to view your History.

2   Tap once on the **Clear** button at the bottom of the panel to clear your search history

Clear

Apple Pay on the Web

Apple Pay is Apple's contactless payment system, which is activated using Touch ID on the iPad or the iPhone. On the iPhone it can be used to make purchases in hundreds of retail outlets, and also online with authorized websites. On the iPad it can only be used for online purchases. To do this:

 Access **Settings > Touch ID & Passcode** and set up your iPad with both of these (see pages 48-49)

 Within **Touch ID & Passcode**, drag these buttons to **On** for the items you want to use with Touch ID

 Select **Settings > Wallet & Apple Pay**

Tap once on the **Add Credit or Debit Card** button

Complete the Apple Pay wizard for the selected credit or debit card (see tip). Once a card has been registered, it can be used to purchase items from participating websites where you see this symbol, or from the iTunes and App Stores, if specified, as in Step 2. Press the Home button to buy an item with Touch ID

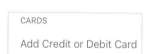

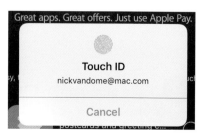

Don't forget

To register a credit or debit card for Apple Pay, enter your name, card number, expiration date and security number. You will then be asked to confirm these details to activate the card. This will be done via a text message or phone call from your card provider, who will supply you with a number to activate the card. Once this is done, the card will be ready to use with Apple Pay.

Card Activated
"Santander Debit Card" is ready for Apple Pay.

8 Staying Organized

An iPad is ideal for all of your organizational needs. This chapter shows how to use the built-in apps to keep fully up-to-date.

Taking Notes

It is always useful to have a quick way of making notes of everyday things, such as shopping lists, recipes or packing lists for traveling. On your iPad, the Notes app is perfect for this function. To use it:

1   Tap once on the **Notes** app

2   Tap once in the text area of a new note to access the keyboard. Start writing the note

Don't forget

Options for formatting text in a note are located here on the Shortcuts bar. If the keyboard is hidden, some of these options appear on the bottom toolbar, colored yellow. This also includes an option for inserting a table into a note, by tapping once on this button.

3   Tap once on this button on the keyboard to hide the keyboard and finish the note. To edit an existing note, tap once on the text and the keyboard will reappear

Don't forget

If iCloud is set up for Notes (check **Notes** is **On** in **Settings** > **Apple ID** > **iCloud**) then all of your notes will be stored here and be available on any other iCloud-enabled devices that you have.

4   As the note is created, it appears in the Notes panel. The most recent note is at the top, and the first line of the note is the title. Tap once on a note to view it

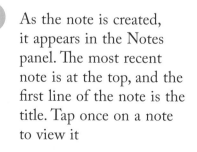

5 Tap once on this button to create a new note

6 Tap once on this button to delete the current note

7 Tap once on this button to share (via social media apps, Mail, Message and other message apps that you have on your iPad) and copy or print a note

8 Tap once on this button to invite people to view and edit a note

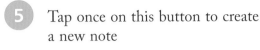

The option in Step 8 can be used to send a link to a note to family or friends via an email or text message. The recipient can then access the note and edit it, as required.

Formatting notes

In iOS 11 the Notes app has a range of text formatting options. To apply formatting to a note:

1 Press and hold next to the piece of text you want to format. Tap on the **Select** button

| Select | Select All | Paste | Insert Drawing | **B** *I* U | Indent Right |

Shopping list
Fish
Red pepper
Pots
Ciabatta

2 Drag the yellow selection handles over the text you want to select

Fish
Red pepper
Pots
Ciabatta
Lemon

3 Tap once on this button to access the formatting options

The formatting options in Step 3 include text styles such as the Title, Heading or Body options, or list options for creating a list from the selection.

125

...cont'd

Notes is one of the apps in which the cursor can be moved (and text selected) by dragging on the screen of the iPad. Tap once on the text area to insert or move the cursor; the cursor can then be positioned by pressing on it and dragging it around the screen. Single words can be selected by double-tapping on them. Once text is selected, the selection can be expanded or contracted by dragging the handles over the screen, in the same way as for moving the cursor.

Tap once on the **Scan Documents** button in Step 8 to scan a document into the Notes app. This is a new feature in iOS 11.

Scan Documents

4. The formatting option selected from Step 3 on page 125 is applied to the selected text (in this instance, a numbered list)

Shopping list

1. Fish
2. Red pepper
3. Pots
4. Ciabatta

5. Tap once on this button to create a checklist from the selected text

6. Radio buttons are added to the list (these are the round buttons to the left-hand side of the text)

○ Fish
○ Red pepper
○ Pots
○ Ciabatta

7. Tap once on the radio buttons to show that an item or a task has been completed

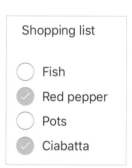

Shopping list

○ Fish
✓ Red pepper
○ Pots
✓ Ciabatta

8. Tap once on this button to add a photo or a video to the note (either by taking one, or from the Photo Library on your iPad)

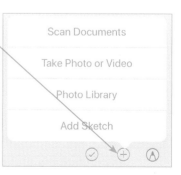

Scan Documents

Take Photo or Video

Photo Library

Add Sketch

Sketching notes

In Notes with iOS 11 there is a Sketch button, which allows you to use your fingers to draw on the note that you are writing. To do this:

1 Tap once on the **Add Sketch** button in Step 8 on the previous page

Add Sketch

2 Select a drawing tool and color at the bottom of the screen, and draw or write on the screen

3 Tap once on the **Done** button

Done   Erase All

in the top left-hand corner to save a sketch; tap once on the Undo button to undo the last action; or tap once on the **Erase All** button to delete a sketch

4 The sketch is added to the current note, and text can also be added in the same way as for any other note

This is my new sketch!

Hot tip

An Apple Pencil can also be used to sketch notes, but this can only be used with the iPad Pro. It can also be used to add Inline Drawings, which are sketches created directly within the note environment, by tapping once on this button at the bottom of the Notes window.

Hot tip

Content can also be shared to Notes from apps such as Safari, Maps and Photos. This creates a note with a link to the appropriate app. To do this, tap once on the **Share** button in an appropriate app and tap once on the **Add to Notes** button.

127

Setting Reminders

Another useful organization app is Reminders. This enables you to create lists for different topics and then set reminders for specific items. A date and time can be set for each reminder, and when this is reached the reminder appears on your iPad screen. To use Reminders:

1 Tap once on the **Reminders** app

2 The Reminder lists are located in the left-hand panel. Tap once on the **New List** button for a list, or **Reminders** to create a new reminder

3 Tap once on a new line and enter the reminder

4 Tap once on the **i** button to access the **Details** window

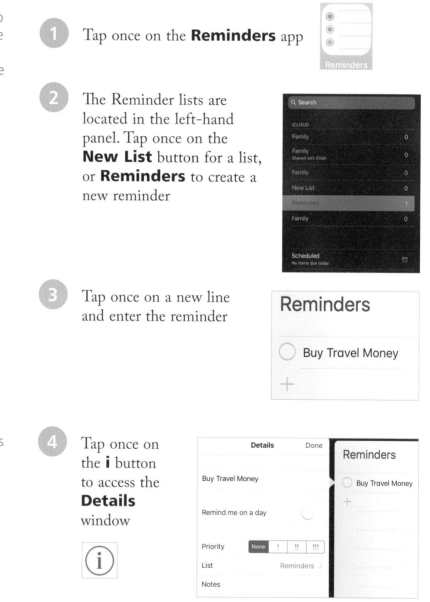

5 Drag this button to **On**

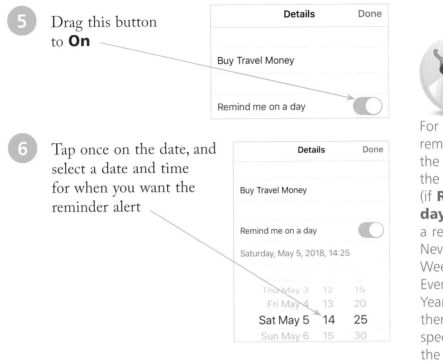

6 Tap once on the date, and select a date and time for when you want the reminder alert

Hot tip

For a recurring reminder, tap once on the **Repeat** link in the **Details** window (if **Remind me on a day** is **On**) and select a repeat option from Never, Every Day, Every Week, Every 2 Weeks, Every Month, or Every Year. The reminder will then appear at the specified timescale, at the time set in Step 6.

129

7 Tap once on the **Done** button

8 On the date and time of the reminder, a pop-up box appears. Drag down here to expand the box

Don't forget

Set the date and time for reminders by dragging up and down on the relevant barrels within the **Details** window. The time can be set in five-minute intervals.

9 Tap once on **Mark as Completed** to close the reminder, or select an option for being reminded about it

Using the Calendar

The built-in iPad calendar can be used to create and view appointments and events. To do this:

The iPad calendar uses continuous scrolling to move through Month view. This means you can view weeks across different months, rather than just viewing each month in its entirety; i.e. you can view the second half of one month and the first half of the next one in the same calendar window.

1 Tap once on the **Calendar** app

2 By default, the calendar is displayed in Month view. Swipe up and down to move between the weeks and months

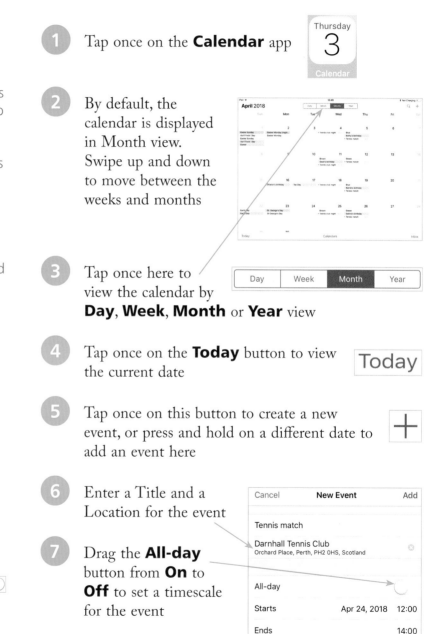

3 Tap once here to view the calendar by **Day**, **Week**, **Month** or **Year** view

| Day | Week | Month | Year |

4 Tap once on the **Today** button to view the current date

Today

5 Tap once on this button to create a new event, or press and hold on a different date to add an event here

$+$

6 Enter a Title and a Location for the event

7 Drag the **All-day** button from **On** to **Off** to set a timescale for the event

Drag the **All-day** button to **On** to set the event for the whole day.

All-day

| Cancel | **New Event** | Add |

Tennis match

Darnhall Tennis Club
Orchard Place, Perth, PH2 0HS, Scotland

All-day

Starts   Apr 24, 2018 12:00

Ends   14:00

8 Tap on the **Starts** and **Ends** dates to set these

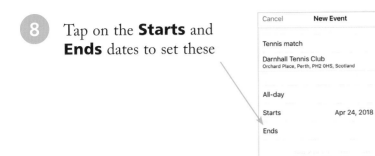

Cancel	New Event	Add

Tennis match

Darnhall Tennis Club
Orchard Place, Perth, PH2 0HS, Scotland

All-day

| Starts | Apr 24, 2018 | 19:00 |
| Ends | | 22:00 |

Sun Apr 22   20   50
Mon Apr 23   21   55
Tue Apr 24   22   00
Wed Apr 25   23   05

Hot tip

A new event can also be created in **Day** view. Press and hold on a time slot to access the **New Event** window.

9 To invite other people to the event, tap once on the **Invitees** link (Calendars needs to be On in iCloud for this function)

Invitees	None >

Hot tip

Tap once on the **Repeat** link in the **New Event** window to set a recurring event, such as a birthday. The repeat options are Every Day, Every Week, Every 2 Weeks, Every Month, or Every Year.

10 Tap once on this button to select a contact from your address book

Cancel	Add Invitees	Done
To:		⊕

11 The contact is added as an invitee for the event

Cancel	Add Invitees	Done
To: Eilidh Vandome,		⊕

12 Tap once on the **Done** button. An email invitation will then be sent to the invitee's email address

13 Tap once on the **Add** button in Step 8 when you have finished entering the details of the event

Don't forget

Select an event as in Step 14, and tap once on the **Delete Event** button at the bottom of the window to remove it.

14 Press and hold on an event, and tap on the **Edit** button to alter the details for the event

Tennis match	Edit
Darnhall Tennis Club	
Orchard Place, Perth, PH2 0HS, Scotland	
Tuesday, Apr 24, 2018	19:00 to 22:00

Delete Event

Your iPad Address Book

There is a built-in address book on your iPad: the Contacts app. This enables you to store contact details, which can then be used to contact people via email, iMessage or FaceTime. To add contacts:

Hot tip

Tap once on a contact's email address to go directly to Mail to send them an email. Tap on the FaceTime video button to access FaceTime for a video call (if the recipient has a compatible device and software for this).

FaceTime

 Tap once on the **Contacts** app

 Tap once on this button to add a new contact

3 Enter the required details for a contact

Cancel	New Contact	Done
add photo	Lucy	
	Vandome	⊗
	Company	
⊖ mobile >	079	
⊕ add phone		

4 Tap once on the **Done** button   Done

 Use these buttons to send a text message, make a call, start a FaceTime video call or send an email

message   call   FaceTime   mail

Don't forget

The details of an individual contact can be shared via email or as an iMessage, using the **Share Contact** button at the bottom of their entry.

Share Contact

6 Tap once on the **Edit** button to edit details in an individual entry   Edit

7 To delete a contact, swipe to the bottom of the window in Edit mode and tap once on the **Delete Contact** button   Delete Contact

Keeping Notified

Although the Notification Center feature is not an app in its own right, it can be used to display information from a variety of apps. The notifications appear as a list of all of the items you want to be reminded about or be made aware of. Notifications are set up within the Settings app. To do this:

1 Tap once on the **Settings** app

2 Tap once on the **Notifications** tab

3 In the **Notification Style** section, tap on an item to determine how it operates when it displays a notification

4 Drag the **Allow Notifications** button to **On** to allow notifications to be displayed for this item

5 Make selections for how you want the notification to appear. This can include sounds for the notifications, showing an app badge and an alert style for the notification

Hot tip

If the **Badge App Icon** is turned **On**, this will display a small, red circle on the app's icon on the Home screen if there are new items to be actioned. For instance, if you have three unread emails, the Mail app will have a small red circle on it, displaying the number 3.

Tap once on the cross next to a notification to dismiss it, or swipe on it from right to left and tap once on the **Clear** button. This is a new feature in iOS 11.

When an item has been removed in Step 5 it appears under the **More Widgets** heading further down the page, and it can be reinstated from here by tapping on the green button that appears next to it.

...cont'd

Viewing notifications

Once the Notifications settings have been selected, they can be used to keep up-to-date with all of your important appointments and reminders, via the Notification Center. There is also a page of useful widgets, which can be customized. To view the Notification Center:

1   Drag down from the top of any screen to view the Notification Center. This displays items that have been selected on the previous page. Tap once on an item to open it in its own app (it then disappears from the Notification Center)

2   Swipe from left to right to view the widgets page

3   Swipe up the page to view all of the items. Tap on one to open it in its own app

4   Tap once on the **Edit** button to specify the items that appear

5   Tap on the red circle next to an item to remove it from appearing on the widgets page, then tap on the **Done** button

Organization Apps

In the App Store there is a wide range of productivity and organization apps. Some of these are:

- **Evernote**. One of the most popular note-taking apps. You can create individual notes and also save them into notebook folders. Evernote works across multiple devices, so if it is installed on other computers or mobile devices, you can access your notes wherever you are.

- **Popplet**. This is a note-taking app that enables you to link notes together, so you can form a mindmap-type creation. You can also include photos and draw pictures.

- **Dropbox**. This is an online service for storing and accessing files. You can upload files from your iPad and then access them from other devices with an internet connection.

- **Bamboo Paper**. This is another note-taking app, but it allows you to do this by handwriting rather than typing. The free version comes with one notebook into which you can put your notes, and the paid-for version provides another 20.

- **Pages**. This is a powerful word processing app that has been developed by Apple. It can be used to create and save documents, which can then be printed or shared via email. There are a number of templates on which documents can be based. There is also a range of formatting and content options.

- **Keynote**. Another Apple productivity app, this is a presentation app that can be used to create slides, which can then be run as a presentation.

- **Numbers**. This is the spreadsheet app that is part of the same suite as Pages and Keynote. Again, templates are provided, or you can create your spreadsheets from scratch to keep track of expenditure or household bills. You can enter formulas into cells to perform simple or complicated calculations.

Most organization apps are found in the **Productivity** category of the App Store.

Other productivity and organization apps to look at include: Notability, Alarmed, Grocery Shopping List, Smart Office, iA Writer, Free Spreadsheet, GoodReader and Wunderlist.

Printing Items

Printing from an iPad has advantages and disadvantages. One advantage is that it is done wirelessly, so you do not have to worry about connecting wires and cables to a printer. The main disadvantage is that not all printers work with the iPad printing system.

AirPrint

Content from an iPad is printed using the AirPrint system that is part of the iOS 11 operating system. This is a wireless printing system that connects to your printer through your Wi-Fi network. However, not all printers are AirPrint- or Wi-Fi-enabled, so it may not work with your current printer.

AirPrint can print content from apps with the Share button, including built-in apps like Safari, Notes, Mail and Photos:

Check on the Apple website for a list of AirPrint-enabled printers: **support. apple.com/en-us/ HT201311**

Apps in the Apple productivity suite of Pages, Numbers and Keynote contain the **Print** button within the **More** options that are accessed from the top toolbar.

1. Tap once on the **Share** button and tap once on the **Print** button

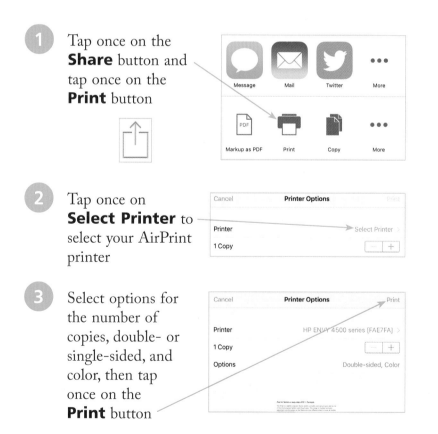

2. Tap once on **Select Printer** to select your AirPrint printer

3. Select options for the number of copies, double- or single-sided, and color, then tap once on the **Print** button

9 Like a Good Book

Your iPad can be used for getting the news, and reading a wide array of books.

The layout of the News app has been updated in iOS 11.

Getting the News

The News app is a news aggregation app that collates news stories from a variety of publications, covering a range of categories. To use the News app:

1 Tap once on the **News** app

2 Tap once on the **Search** button to select topics to populate the news feed

3 Enter a topic to search for, and tap once on an item to add it. This can be general topics or specific subjects

4 Tap once on the **Following** button on the bottom toolbar to view the items that were added in Step 3

5 Tap on the **For You** button to view the news feed from selected publications and subjects. Tap on the main heading (Top Stories, etc.) to view all of the items for that category

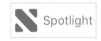

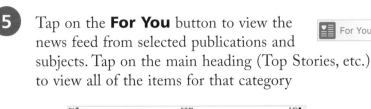

6 Scroll down the main For You page to view top trending topics within the News app

Tap once on the **Spotlight** button on the bottom toolbar to view in-depth articles about topics in which you have identified an interest in the News app.

7 When an article has been opened for reading, tap on these buttons on the top toolbar to, from left to right: move back to the previous page, share the item (or save it), unfollow a news topic so you see fewer items, follow a news topic for more similar items, or change the font size

8 Items that are saved using the Share button (see above) can be viewed in the **Saved** section

Finding Books

For anyone interested in reading, the iPad removes the need to carry around a lot of bulky books. Whether you are at home or traveling, you can keep hundreds of digital books (ebooks) on your iPad. This is done with the iBooks app, which can be used to download and read books across most genres; it is your own portable library. To use iBooks:

Tap on the drop-down arrow at the top of **My Books** and select **All Books**, then tap on the **New Collection** button to create new shelves under specific headings. These can be used to store books according to genre. Swipe left and right to move between collections.

To add books to a collection, tap on the **Select** button and tap on a book. Then, tap on the **Move** button and select the collection into which you want to move the item.

Books can be searched for in a similar way as searching for apps. See page 91 for more details.

 Tap once on the **iBooks** app

 The iBooks app opens the iBooks Store at **My Books**, which consists of your Library (bookcase), which initially is empty, and then displays items that you have downloaded

Tap once on the **Featured** button and navigate through the iBooks Store in the same way as the App Store to find the required titles

 Use the buttons on the bottom toolbar to search for items within the iBooks Store, under **Featured**, **Top Charts**, **Top Authors** and **Purchased**

Downloading Books

Once you have identified appropriate books, they can then be downloaded to the **My Books** section of the iBooks app. To do this:

 Tap once on the book image or title to view its details

 View the details of the book and any reviews (under the **Reviews** heading)

 Tap once on this button to download a sample of the book

SAMPLE

 Tap once on the price (or Free) button to purchase and download the book

£1.99

 Downloaded books appear in the **My Books** section of the iBooks app. Tap once on a book cover to open it and start reading

Under the **Related** heading in Step 2, you will find details of similar books to the one being viewed.

Reading Books

Reading an iBook

Once you have opened an iBook there are a number of ways to navigate and work with the content:

Hot tip

To hide the toolbar, tap once on a page.

Don't forget

The Table of Contents can be used to view bookmarks and notes (see next page) that have been added to pages. From the Table of Contents page, tap once on the **Resume** button to return to the page you were looking at.

Don't forget

If you are viewing a sample version of a book, there is a **Buy** button on the top toolbar. Tap once on this to buy the full version of the book.

1 Tap once in the middle of a page in an iBook to access the top toolbar

2 Tap once on this button to return to the iBooks **Library** (bookcase)

3 Tap once on this button to view the Table of Contents

4 Tap once on this button to change the text size, font or color

5 Tap once on this button to search for an item in the book

6 Tap once on this button to bookmark a page

7 Drag on this bottom bar to move through the book

Working with text

When you are reading an iBook there are a number of options for enhancing the reading experience, from looking up dictionary definitions of words to making notes about the text. To do this:

1 Press and hold on a word to highlight it and access the text toolbar

| Look Up | Highlight | Note | Search |

...he had tried to say something. He had lis-tiently to the inarticulate sounds emerg-

2 Tap once on the **Look Up** button to access a dictionary definition for the selected word, and suggested related websites, videos and apps. At the bottom of the window there is also an option for searching over the web

inarticulate | ɪnɑːˈtɪkjʊlət | adjective

3 Highlight a word and drag on each of the blue markers to extend the highlighted area

| Highlight | Note | Search |

THE RAIN DID not stop first thing. Nor second thing. In fact, it didn't stop at all. It was mild and wet week upon week. The ground was saturated, European motorways caved in, migratory birds did not migrate and there were reports of insects hitherto unseen in northern climes. The calendar showed that it was winter but Oslo's parkland

Hot tip

Tap once on the **Search** button in Step 1 to see where a selected word or phrase appears throughout the book.

Beware

If you click on one of the suggestions in Step 2, this takes you away from the iBook page.

Hot tip

Tap once on the **Note** button in Step 3 to add a note about the selected text.

Hot tip

Tap once on the **Highlight** button in Step 3 to highlight the selected text with a specific color.

Kindle on your iPad

The Kindle is a popular eReader device for reading ebooks. It is possible to use the Kindle app on your iPad to download Kindle books to it:

When you first access the Kindle on your iPad you will be asked if you want to access titles that you have previously downloaded to your Kindle. After this, they will appear in the Cloud section.

You can delete a title from the **Device** section by tapping and holding on the cover and then tapping on the **Remove from Device** button. However, the title remains in the Cloud section and can be downloaded again.

If you download a book from the Kindle Cloud, it only appears in the Kindle app and not in your iBooks app.

 1 Download the Kindle app from the Books category in the App Store

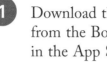

 2 Tap once on this button to open the **Kindle** app

 3 If you have an Amazon account, enter the details here to register the Kindle app through your iPad. If you do not have an Amazon account, one can be obtained from the Amazon website

 4 Tap once on the **Cloud** button to view the titles that are in the Kindle Cloud, i.e. in your Kindle account on Amazon

 5 Tap once on a title to download it from the Kindle Cloud to your iPad

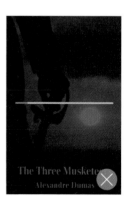

 6 Tap once on the **Device** button to view items that have been downloaded to your iPad

10 Leisure Time

The possibilities for enjoyment from your iPad are huge. This chapter looks at downloading and listening to music, and capturing and using photos and videos in creative ways. It also covers some lifestyle opportunities and shows how you can obtain apps related to art, health and cookery.

Buying Music and More

As well as using Apple Music, music on the iPad can also be bought, downloaded and played using the iTunes Store, using your Apple ID with credit or debit card details added. Music can then also be played via the Music app:

Don't forget

If you have iTunes on another computer, you can synchronize the music (and other items) that you have there with your iPad. To do this, attach the iPad to your computer (with the Lightning connector to USB cable). Click on the icon below to access the **Summary** details for the iPad. Under the **Options** section, check Off the **Sync this iPad over Wi-Fi** checkbox and check On the **Manually manage music and videos** checkbox. Click on the required headings in the left-hand panel of the iTunes window to manually sync the required items (this can include additional items to music and videos, e.g. apps and books).

1 Tap once on the **iTunes Store** app

2 Tap once on the **Music** button on the iTunes toolbar at the bottom of the window

3 Scroll up and down to view the featured items, or tap once on the **Genres** button to find items this way

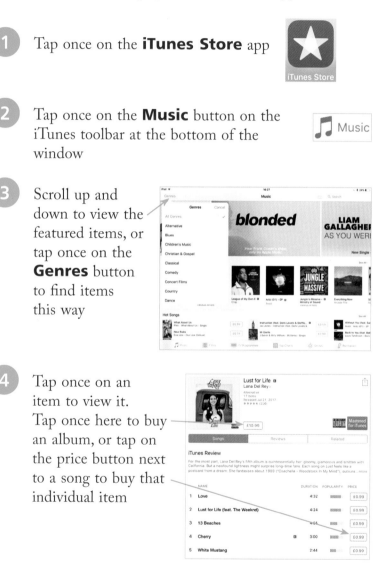

4 Tap once on an item to view it. Tap once here to buy an album, or tap on the price button next to a song to buy that individual item

5 Purchased items are included in the Music app's Library (see page 148) as well as the iTunes Library, from where they can be downloaded again at any time to the iPad or any other Apple devices you have

...cont'd

Around the iTunes Store

In addition to music, there is a wide range of other content that can be downloaded from the iTunes Store:

1 Tap once on the **Films (Movies)** button to view the latest movie releases

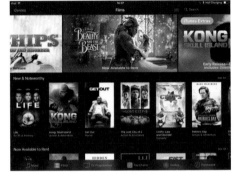

2 Tap once on the **TV Programmes (TV Shows)** button to view the latest TV releases

3 Tap once on the **Top Charts** button on the bottom toolbar to view the top selling items for music, movies and TV

4 Tap once on the **Genius** button on the bottom toolbar to view suggestions made by iTunes based on your previous purchases

5 Tap once on the **Purchased** button on the bottom toolbar to view all of your previous purchases from the iTunes Store

Scroll up and down to view the content on the Homepage for Movies and TV. Swipe left and right on individual panels to view the items in each section. Tap once on the **See All** button at the top of a panel, e.g. Recent Releases, to view all of the items within it.

Since all items that you buy and download from the iTunes Store are kept within the Purchased section, if you ever delete or lose an item you can download it again, for free, from this section. Tap once on the cloud icon next to an item to download it again.

Playing Music

Once music has been bought from the iTunes Store it can be played on your iPad using the Music app. To do this:

 Tap once on the **Music** app

 Tap once on the **Library** button on the bottom toolbar

3 The items in the music Library are displayed. By default, this is organized by **Recently Added**

To create a Playlist of songs, tap once on the **Playlists** button (from the **Library** list in Step 4), then tap once on the **New** button. Give it a name, and then you can add songs from your Library.

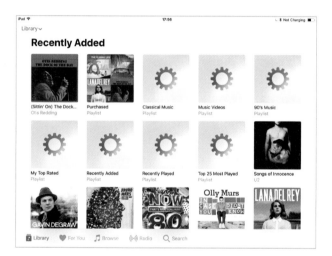

4 Tap once on the **Library** button in the top left-hand corner. Select one of the options for viewing items in the Library. This can be **Playlists**, **Artists**, **Albums**, **Songs** or **Downloaded Music**

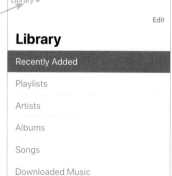

5 For the **Artists** section, tap once on an artist in the left-hand panel to view the related items in the right-hand panel

6 Tap once on an item in the right-hand panel to view its details. The tracks from the album are displayed

7 Tap once on a track to play it. Limited options for the music controls are displayed at the bottom of the window

The **Albums** section displays thumbnails of each album. Tap on one to view its contents. The **Songs** section displays a list of all of the individual songs within the Library. **Downloaded Music** has the same sections for downloaded music as for the main Library.

149

By default, music that has been bought from the iTunes Store is kept online and can be played on your iPad by streaming it online over Wi-Fi. However, it is also possible to download tracks to your iPad so that you can play them without being online. Tap once on this button to download a track:

...cont'd

8 Tap here to view details of a track

9 The details of the track are displayed. Use these buttons to rewind, pause/play and fast-forward the track

Hot tip

Music controls including Play, Fast Forward, Rewind and Volume can also be applied in the **Control Center**, which can be accessed by swiping up from the bottom of the Home screen, or swiping up twice from within any app.

10 Tap once here to access the menu for the currently-playing track. This includes downloading the song onto your iPad, deleting it, adding it to a playlist or sharing it

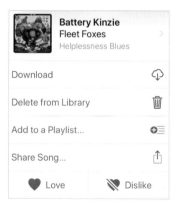

Starting with Apple Music

Apple Music is a service that makes the entire Apple iTunes library of music available to users. It is a subscription service, payable on a monthly basis. Music can be streamed over the internet, or downloaded so you can listen to it when you are offline. To start with Apple Music:

1 Tap once on the **Music** app

2 Tap once on the **For You** button

3 Initially, there is an option for a 3-month free trial of Apple Music. After you have used this, you will have to choose a paid-for option. Tap once on the **Choose Your Plan** button

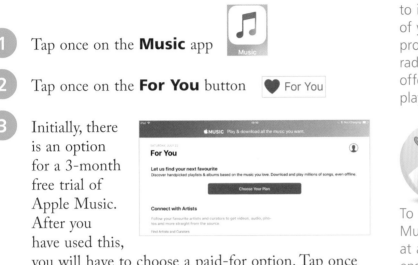

4 Select either an **Individual**, **Family** or a **University Student** membership plan, and tap once on the **Join Apple Music** button

5 Enter your **Apple ID Password** (an Apple ID is required in order to use Apple Music) and tap once on the **Continue** button

Apple Music has been redesigned for iOS 11 to improve the layout of your music Library, provide a range of radio stations, and offer hand-picked playlists.

Hot tip

To end your Apple Music subscription at any point (and to ensure you do not subscribe at the end of the free trial) open the **Settings** app. Tap once on the **iTunes & App Store** option and tap once on your own **Apple ID** link (in blue). Tap once on the **View Apple ID** button, and under **Subscriptions** tap once on the **Manage** button. Drag the **Automatic Renewal** button to **Off**. You can then renew your Apple Music membership, if required, by selecting one of the **Renewal Options**.

The camera on the back of the iPad is an iSight one, and is capable of capturing high-resolution photos and also high-definition videos. The front-facing one is better for video calls and "selfies" (photos of yourself).

Hot tip

Tap once on this button on the top camera toolbar to take a Live Photo, which is a short, animated video, in GIF file format.

Hot tip

Photos can also be taken by pressing the **Volume** button on the side of the iPad.

Taking Photos and Videos

Because of its mobility and the quality of the screen, the iPad is excellent for taking and displaying photos. Photos can be captured directly using one of the two built-in cameras (one on the front and one on the back) and then viewed, edited and shared using the Photos app. To do this:

1 Tap once on the **Camera** app

2 Tap once on the shutter button to capture a photo

3 Tap once on this button to swap between the front and back cameras on the iPad

The iPad cameras can be used for different formats:

1 Swipe up or down at the side of the camera screen, underneath the shutter button, to access the different shooting options. Tap once on the **Photo** button to capture photos at full-screen size. Tap once on the **Square** button to capture photos at this ratio

2 Swipe down, and tap once on the **Time-Lapse** button or the **Slo-Mo** button to access these options. For a time-lapse image, the camera keeps taking photos periodically until you press the shutter button again

3 Tap once on the **Video** button, and press the red shutter button to take a video. Press the shutter button again to stop recording

Camera Settings

iCloud sharing

Certain camera options can be applied within Settings. Several of these are to do with storing and sharing your photos via iCloud. To access these:

1 Tap once on the **Settings** app

2 Tap once on the **Photos** tab

3 Drag the **iCloud Photo Library** button to **On** to upload your whole photo Library from your iPad to the iCloud (it remains on your iPad too). Similarly, photos on your other Apple devices can also be uploaded to the iCloud (see first tip)

> iCloud Photo Library

4 Select an option for storing iCloud photos. (**Optimize iPad Storage** uses less storage as it uses smaller file sizes of your images)

> Optimize iPad Storage ✓
> Download and Keep Originals

5 Drag the **My Photo Stream** button to **On** to enable all new photos and videos that you take on your iPad to be uploaded automatically to the iCloud, via Wi-Fi

> My Photo Stream

6 Drag the **iCloud Photo Sharing** button to **On** to allow you to create albums within the Photos app that can then be shared with other people via iCloud (see page 59)

> iCloud Photo Sharing

If the **iCloud Photo Library** option is **On** then your photos will all appear in the **All Photos** album in the Albums section, as well as in the Photos section. If the iCloud Photo Library is **Off** there will be a **Camera Roll** album in the Albums section, where photos created on your iPad will appear.

153

In the **Camera** Settings, drag the **Grid** button to **On** to place a grid over the screen when you are taking photos with the camera, if required. This can be used to help compose photos by placing subjects using the grid.

Viewing Photos

Once photos have been captured, they can be viewed and organized in the Photos app. To do this:

1 Tap once on the **Photos** app

2 At the top level, all photos are displayed according to the years in which they were taken

3 Tap once within the **Years** window to view photos according to specific, more defined, timescales. This is the **Collections** level. Tap once on the **Years** button to move back up one level

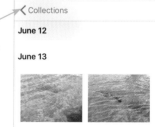

4 Tap once within the **Collections** window to drill further into the photos, within the **Moments** window. Tap once on the **Collections** button to go back up one level

5 Tap once on a photo within the **Moments** window to view it at full size. Tap once on the **Moments** button to go back up one level

Viewing Memories

The Photos app also has a section where the best of your photos are selected and displayed automatically. To use this:

 Tap once on the **Memories** button on the bottom toolbar

The Photos app automatically collates photos into groups of memories, based on criteria such as location, people, Best of the Year, and Best of Last 3 Months. Tap once on a memory to view the photos within it

Tap once on this button to view a memory of photos as a movie (slideshow). Tap once on the movie to access the control buttons at the bottom of the screen for specifying the style and speed of the movie

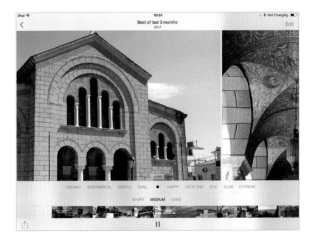

155

Hot tip

The **Memories** section is a great way to view the best of your photos from a trip or a vacation, without having to sort through them yourself.

Don't forget

Tap once on the **Edit** button in Step 3 to access settings to customize the movie, including editing the movie's title, and specifying the title image, the music and the movie's duration.

Creating Albums

Within the Photos app it is possible to create different albums in which you can store photos. This can be a good way to organize them according to different categories and headings. To do this:

1 Tap once on the **Albums** button on the bottom toolbar of the Photos app

Albums

2 Tap once on this button

3 Enter a name for the new album

New Album
Enter a name for this album.

Zante

Cancel   Save

4 Tap once on the **Save** button

5 Tap on the photos you want to include in the album

Select All   Add 5 photos to "Zante".

June 13

6 Tap once on the **Done** button

Done

7 The new album is added to the Albums section in the Photos app

My Albums

Zante
5

Selecting Photos

It is easy to take hundreds or thousands of digital photos, and most of the time you will only want to use a selection of them. Within the Photos app it is possible to select individual photos so that you can share them, delete them or add them to albums.

1 Access the Moments section and tap once on the **Select** button

Select

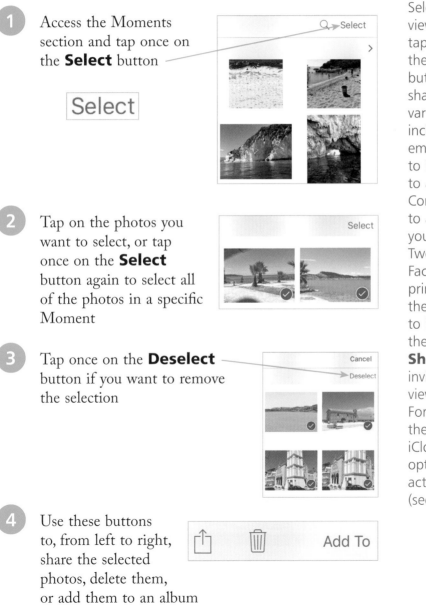

2 Tap on the photos you want to select, or tap once on the **Select** button again to select all of the photos in a specific Moment

3 Tap once on the **Deselect** button if you want to remove the selection

4 Use these buttons to, from left to right, share the selected photos, delete them, or add them to an album

Hot tip

Select a photo (or view it at full size) and tap once on the **Share** button to share it in a variety of ways. These include: messaging; emailing; sending to iCloud; adding to a contact in your Contacts app; adding to a Note; using as your iPad wallpaper; Tweeting; sending to Facebook or Flickr; and printing and copying the photo. For sharing to iCloud, tap once on the **iCloud Photo Sharing** option, to invite other people to view your photo(s). For iCloud sharing, the iCloud Library and iCloud Photo Sharing options have to be activated for iCloud (see page 153).

iCloud Photo Sharing

157

Beware

Editing changes are made to the original photo once the changes have been saved. These will also apply to any albums into which the photo has been placed.

Hot tip

If faces are detected in a photo, the Red Eye button is available. Tap once on this, and tap on any faces with red eyes to remove it.

Don't forget

Most photos benefit from some cropping, to enhance the main subject and give it greater prominence.

Editing Photos

The Photos app has options to perform some basic photo-editing operations. To use these:

1 Open a photo at full-screen size and tap once on the **Edit** button

2 The editing buttons are located on the right-hand side of the screen. Tap once on the **Auto Enhance** button to apply one-touch editing improvements

3 Tap once on the **Smart Composition** button and drag the resizing handles to crop your photo

4 Drag the dial at the right of the photo to rotate it by degrees (straighten it)

5 Tap once on the **Filters** button to select special effects to be applied to the photo

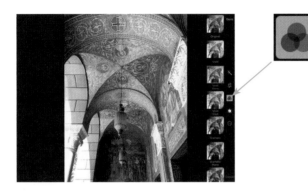

Live Photos can also be edited in the Photos app – this is a new feature for iPads using iOS 11.

6 Tap once on the **Smart Adjustments** button to select color-editing options. Select the option and apply the effect, as required

Hot tip

The Photo Booth app is a good one to use with grandchildren, who will enjoy experimenting with its fun and special effects. Open the app, select one of the effects and take the photo in the same way as for a standard one.

159

7 For each function, tap once on the **Done** button to save the photo with the selected changes

Done

Photo Booth

8 Tap once on the **Cancel** button and tap once on **Discard Changes** to cancel any edits you have made

Discard Changes

Cancel

Viewing Videos

The Videos app can be used to download and view video content from the iTunes Store, rather than viewing your own videos (which is done through the Photos app). To do this:

1 Tap once on the **Videos** app

2 The Videos app is initially empty of content. Tap once on the **Store** button to access video content in the **iTunes Store**

3 Tap once on the **Movies** (or **Films**) button or the **TV Shows** (or **TV Programmes**) button

4 Tap once on an item to review its content. Tap once here to download it. This is usually in the form of buying or renting a video

5 The downloaded video appears in the Videos app. Tap once on the cover to view its contents

6 Tap once here to play a video

Art and Drawing

Viewing art

It is always a pleasure to view works of art in real life, but the next best alternative is to be able to look at them on the high-resolution Retina Display on your iPad. As far as viewing art goes, there are two options:

- Using apps that contain general information about museums and art galleries.

- Using apps that display the works belonging to museums and art galleries.

In general, type the name of a museum or art gallery into the App Store Search box to see if there is an applicable app.

Creating pictures

If you want to branch out from just looking at works of art, you can try creating some of your own too. There is a range of drawing and painting apps that can be used to let your creative side run riot. Most of these function in a similar fashion in terms of creating pictures, with drawing tools that you can select and then use to create a drawing by using your finger on the screen (or an Apple Pencil on the iPad Pro). Most drawing apps also have an Undo function and an Eraser to remove unwanted items. Some apps to try are:

- **Brushes Redux**. One of the most powerful painting apps with a wide range of tools and features, including up to six layers in each painting and five blend modes.

- **Drawing Pad**. Similar to Brushes, but not at such a high level. Suitable as a starter option for iPad painting.

- **Inspire Pro**. A wide range of blending features makes this one of the best painting apps around.

- **How to Draw Everything**. A drawing app that has tutorials for learning how to draw, and also examples that can be used as templates and copied over.

- **SketchBook Express for iPad**. A sketching app at a similar level to Brushes Redux, for painting.

Hot tip

Most top museums have some form of app available. If there is not one for a museum in which you are interested, try contacting the museum and ask if they are planning on developing an app.

Hot tip

If you cannot find a certain app in the search results in the App Store, tap once on the **Filters** button, to the left of the Search box, and select the **Supports > iPhone Only** option. These apps can be downloaded for the iPad too, although they will have a smaller screen area to view the app.

If you are using your iPad in the kitchen, keep it away from direct contact with cooking areas, to avoid splashes and possible damage. If there is a risk of this, cover the iPad with clingfilm/plastic wrap to give it some protection.

Many recipe apps have a facility for uploading your own recipes, so that they can be shared with other people.

Cooking with your iPad

Your iPad may not be quite clever enough to cook dinner for you, but there are enough cookery apps to ensure that you will never go without a good meal with your iPad at your side. Some to look at are:

- **Allrecipes Dinner Spinner**. Instead of just reading recipes, use this app to watch them being made in step-by-step videos.

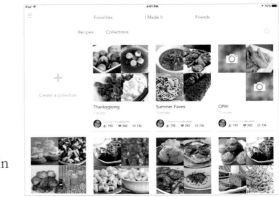

- **Change4Life Smart Recipes**. Over 160 healthy and tasty recipes for all meals throughout the day. There are also options for creating shopping lists and saving favorite recipes that you have created.

- **BigOven 350,000+ Recipes and Grocery List**. As the name suggests, thousands of recipes to keep you busy in the kitchen for as long as you want. You can also store your grocery lists here.

- **Cake Recipes**. To get your mouth watering, this app has hundreds of cake ideas, from the simple to the exotic.

- **Green Kitchen**. A must for vegetarians, with stylish and creative recipes for organic and vegetarian food.

- **Jamie Oliver's Recipes**. An app featuring the recipes of the well-known chef Jamie Oliver. (Most well-known chefs now have their own cooking apps: just enter the name of a chef in the App Store to see the options.)

- **Healthy Slow Cooker Recipes**. Put your dish together with this app, leave it in the slow cooker, and then enjoy it several hours later when ready.

Staying Healthy

Most people are more health-conscious these days, and usefully the App Store has a category covering Health & Fitness. This includes apps about general fitness, healthy eating, relaxation and yoga. Some to try are:

- **Calorie Counter & Diet Tracker**. If you want to stick to a diet, this app can help you along the way. You need to register, which is free, and then you can set your own diet plan and fitness profile.

- **Daily Workouts**. Some of the exercise apps are for dedicated gym-goers. If you are looking for something a bit less extreme, this app could fit the bill. A range of easy-to-follow exercises that will keep you fit.

- **Daily Yoga**. Audio and video instructions for timed sessions, and over 30 yoga poses.

- **Menu Planner**. A dieting aid that enables you to create your own menu plans.

- **My Pilates Guru**. Use this app to work through over 80 Pilates exercise sessions. You can also create your own sessions and save them to repeat.

- **Relax Melodies**. Over 50 sound files to help you relax or fall asleep. Different melodies can be combined to create a customized soundtrack to help you get to sleep.

- **Sleep Pillow Sounds**. Everyone enjoys a good night's sleep, and this app can help you achieve it. A collection of ambient sounds are played to help you relax and sleep.

- **Universal Breathing Exercise Timer**. Designed to promote slow breathing, to enhance relaxation and general health.

Don't forget

There is also a **Medical** category in the App Store that contains a range of apps covering varied medical topics and subjects.

Beware

The version of iOS 11 for the iPhone also has a built-in Health app. However, this is not provided with the iPad, as it is designed to work with the iPhone and the Apple Watch. Find out more in our companion book **iPhone & Apple Watch for Health & Fitness in easy steps**.

Beware

If you have a genuine medical complaint, get it checked out by your doctor, rather than searching online.

Playing Games

Although computer games may seem like the preserve of the younger generation, this is definitely not the case. Not all computer games are of the shoot-em-up or racing variety, and the App Store also contains puzzles and versions of popular board games. Some games to try are:

- **Chess**. Pit your wits against this Chess app. Various settings can be applied for each game, such as the level of difficulty.

- **Checkers**. Similar to the Chess app, but for Checkers (Draughts). Hints are also available to help develop your skills and knowledge.

- **Mahjong**. A version of the popular Chinese game, this is a matching game for single players, rather than playing with other people.

- **Scrabble**. An iPad version of the best-selling word game that can be played with up to four people.

- **Solitaire**. An old favorite, the card game where you have to build sequences and remove all of the cards.

- **Sudoku**. The logic game where you have to fill different grids with numbers 1-9, without having any of the same number in a row or column.

- **Tetris**. One of the original computer games, where you have to piece together falling shapes to make lines.

- **Words With Friends**. Similar to Scrabble, an online word game, played with other users.

Don't forget

As well as the games here, there is a full range of other types of games in the App Store, which can be accessed from the **Games** button on the bottom toolbar of the App Store.

11 Traveling Companion

This chapter shows how the iPad is an essential travel accessory, ideal when you are on the move. This chapter looks at the Maps app for getting around, and a range of travel apps.

To ensure that the Maps app works most effectively, it has to be enabled in Location Services so that it can use your current location (**Settings** > **Privacy** > **Location Services** > **Maps** and select **While Using the App** under **Allow Location Access**).

Hot tip

Tap on the icon in Step 2 to change it into the active compass, below. With this activated, when you change position the map moves with you at the same time.

Looking Around Maps

With the Maps app, you need never again wonder about where a location is, or worry about getting directions to somewhere. As long as you are connected to Wi-Fi or have a 3G/4G network, you will be able to do the following:

- Search maps around the world.
- Find addresses, famous buildings or landmarks.
- Get directions between different locations.
- View traffic conditions.

Viewing maps

To view your current location and maps around the world:

 Tap once on the **Maps** app

 Tap once on this button to view your current location

3 Double-tap on a map with one finger to zoom in (or swipe outwards with thumb and forefinger)

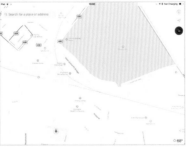

4 Tap once with two fingers on a map to zoom out (or pinch inwards with thumb and forefinger)

Finding Locations

Within Maps you can search for addresses, locations, landmarks or businesses. To do this:

1 The Search box is at the top of the window

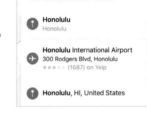

2 Enter an item into the Search box. As you type, suggestions appear underneath. Tap on one to go to that location

3 The location is shown on the map, and there is information about it in the left-hand panel

4 For your current location, categories for searching over items such as food outlets, shops and entertainment are available when you first tap in the Search box. Tap on one of these to see results for that category in the current location, and tap on specific items to view their own details

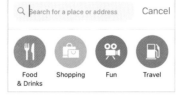

Tap on the **i** button in the top right-hand corner of any map, to access the Maps Settings. This can be used to display the default map style and also **Transit** and **Satellite**.

You can also search for locations by postcode or zip code.

Some locations provide a 3D Flyover tour. If this is available, a **Flyover** button will be displayed in Step 3.

Getting Directions

Finding your way around is an important element of using maps. This can be done with the Directions function:

1 Tap once in the Search box at the top of the window

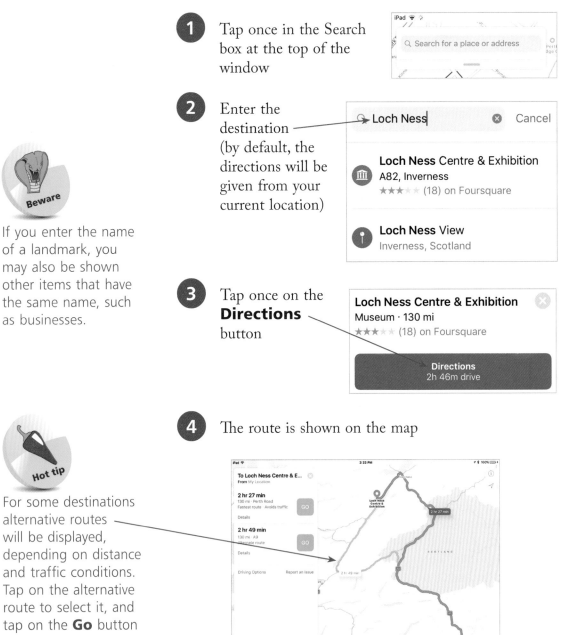

Beware

If you enter the name of a landmark, you may also be shown other items that have the same name, such as businesses.

2 Enter the destination (by default, the directions will be given from your current location)

3 Tap once on the **Directions** button

4 The route is shown on the map

Hot tip

For some destinations alternative routes will be displayed, depending on distance and traffic conditions. Tap on the alternative route to select it, and tap on the **Go** button to proceed.

5 Tap on each of these buttons at the bottom of the window to view the route for **Drive**, **Walk** or **Transit** using an appropriate app

6 Tap once on the **Go** button to start the directions and view step-by-step instructions on the map

GO

7 The route is displayed, starting from your current location. Audio instructions tell you the directions to be followed. As you follow the route, the map and instructions are updated

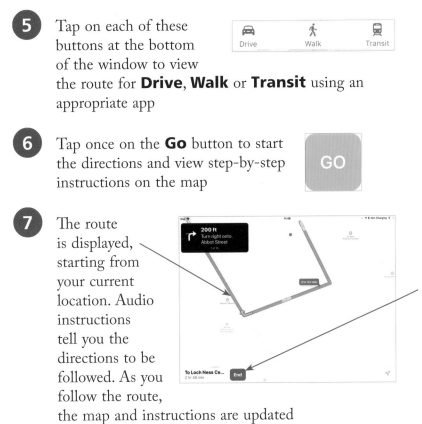

169

8 Swipe up from here to access options for the **Overview** or **Details** of the route. The Details option provides a step-by-step view of the route

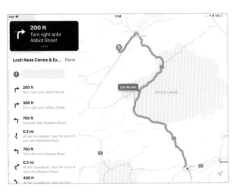

Traveling with your iPad

When you go traveling, there are a few essentials that you have to consider: passport, money and insurance, to name three. To this you can add your iPad: it is a perfect traveling companion that can help you plan your trip and keep you informed and entertained when you are away from home.

Uses for traveling

There are a lot of App Store apps that can be used for different aspects of traveling. However, the built-in apps can also be put to good use before and during your travels:

Hot tip

The Clock app can also be used to keep an eye on the time in different parts of the world; set alarms; and as a stopwatch and timer.

170

Beware

You can also use the Videos app to download movies and TV shows from the iTunes Store. However, these will take up a significant amount of space on your iPad in terms of storage.

- **Notes**. Create lists of items to pack or landmarks that you want to visit.

- **Contacts**. Keep your Contacts app up-to-date so that you can use it to send postcards to friends and family. You can also use it to access phone numbers if you want to phone home.

- **Reminders**. Set reminders for important tasks such as changing foreign currency and buying tickets, and for details of flights.

- **Music**. Use this app to play your favorite music while you are traveling or relaxing at your destination.

- **Photos**. Store photos of your trip with this app and play them back as a slideshow when you get home.

- **FaceTime**. If you have a Wi-Fi connection at your destination you will be able to keep in touch using video calls (as long as the recipient has FaceTime too).

- **iBooks**. Instead of dragging lots of heavy books around, use this app as your vacation library.

Planning your Trip

A lot of the fun and excitement of going on vacation and traveling is in the planning. The anticipation of researching new places to visit and explore can whet the appetite for what is ahead. The good news is, you can plan your whole itinerary while sitting in an armchair with your iPad on your lap. In the App Store there are apps for organizing your itinerary, and others for exploring the possibilities of where you can go:

TripIt

This is an app for keeping all of your travel details in one place. You have to register, which is free, and you can then enter your own itinerary details. Whenever you receive an email confirmation for a flight, hotel or car hire that you have booked, you can email this to your TripIt account and this will be added to your itinerary.

GetPacked

A great way to get peace of mind before you leave. This app generates a packing list and to-do lists to check before you leave, based on questions that you answer about your vacation and travel arrangements. You can then select items to include on your packing list, from clothes to documents and medical items.

Don't forget

Although there is a small fee for the GetPacked app, it is well worth it, as it covers everything you will need to consider before you leave.

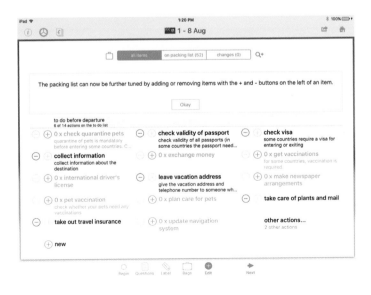

...cont'd

Cool Escapes Hotels & Resorts

Guaranteed to give you itchy feet, this app matches quality hotels with some amazing locations around the world. You can explore by map, country, area, hotel type and price to find the perfect combination.

172

Some map apps are free to download but then there is a fee to buy some of the associated maps.

World Atlas and world map

A comprehensive travel companion that offers a world atlas containing information about countries, cities, landmarks, airports and events. Navigate around the atlas with the same swiping and tapping gestures as the Maps app. Tap on an item to access a wealth of information about it.

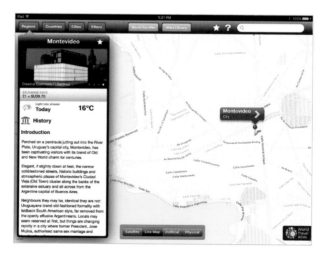

Viewing Flights

Flying is a common part of modern travel, and although you do not have to book separate flights for a vacation (if it is part of a package) there are a number of apps for booking flights and also following the progress of those in the air:

Skyscanner
This app can be used to find flights at airports around the world. Enter your details such as the departure airport, destination and dates of travel. The results show a range of available options, covering different price ranges.

Flightradar24
If you like viewing the paths of flights that are in the air, or need to check if flights are going to be delayed, this app provides this real-time information. Flights are shown according to flight number and airline.

Flight apps need to have an internet connection in order to show real-time flight information.

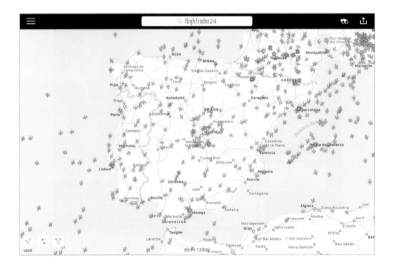

FlightAware Flight Tracker
Another app for tracking flights, showing arrivals and departures and also information about delays.

Finding Hotels

The internet is a perfect vehicle for finding good-value hotel rooms around the world. When hotels have spare capacity, this can quickly be relayed to associated websites, where users can usually benefit from cheap prices and special offers. There are plenty of apps that have details of thousands of hotels around the world, such as:

TripAdvisor

One of the top travel apps, this not only has hotel information but also restaurants, activities and flights. Enter a destination in the Search box and then navigate through the available options.

Hotels.com

A stylish app that enables you to enter search keywords for finding hotels based on destination, hotel name or nearby landmarks.

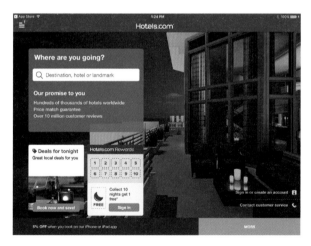

Booking.com

Another good, fully-featured hotel app that provides a comprehensive service and excellent prices.

lastminute.com

An app that specializes in getting the best prices by dealing with rooms that are available at short notice. Some genuine bargains can be found here, for hotels of all categories.

Hot tip

When booking flights and hotels, look up the price on your iPad, but check it on another, non-Apple, devices too, e.g. a Windows computer. Sometimes, different prices are displayed for searches from different types of devices.

Hot tip

Most hotel apps have reviews of all of the listed establishments. It is always worth reading these, as it gives you views from the people who have actually been there.

Converting Currency

Money is always important in life, and never more so than when you are on vacation and possibly following a budget. It is therefore imperative to know the exchange rate of currencies in different countries compared with your own. Two apps that provide this service are:

XE Currency

This app delivers information about exchange rates for all major world currencies and also a wealth of background information, such as high and low rates and historical charts.

When changing currency, either at home or abroad, always shop around to get the best rate. Using credit cards abroad usually attracts a supplementary charge too.

Currency

This app provides up-to-date exchange rates for over 150 currencies and 100 countries.

If you cannot find a certain app in the search results in the App Store, tap once on the **Filters** button, to the left of the Search box, and select the **Supports > iPhone Only** option. These apps can be downloaded for the iPad too, although they will have a smaller screen area to view the app.

There are several travel apps that have the functionality to mark locations around the world that you have visited. In the **Travel** section of the App Store, enter **places visited** (or similar) into the Search box, to view the matching apps.

Travel Apps

Everyone has different priorities and preferences when they are on vacation. The following are some apps from the App Store that cover a range of activities and services:

- **Cities of the World Photo Quiz**. An app to stimulate your wanderlust, with photo quizzes for recognizing over 110 famous cities. There are different types of quizzes, and also flashcards that provide the answers for you.

- **Florida State Parks Guide – Pocket Ranger**. An extensive guide to the outdoor attractions of the Florida State Parks, including general information about all of the parks, advanced GPS maps and built-in compass.

- **Google Earth**. Not just a travel aid, this app enables you to search the globe and look at photos and 3D maps of all your favorite places.

- **Great App to Disneyland Paris**. If you are entertaining your grandchildren at Disneyland Paris, this app will help you survive the experience. Maps, show times and descriptions of features help you organize all aspects of your visit.

- **Kayak**. A useful all-round app that compares hundreds of travel websites to get the best prices for flights, hotels and car rental. You can also create your own itineraries.

- **Language apps**. If you want to learn a new language for your travels, there is a wide range of apps to do this. These are located in either the Travel or Education categories in the App Store.

- **London Tube Map**. Find your way around London with this digital version of the iconic Tube Map. It includes live departure boards and station information.

- **Magnifying Glass with Light**. Not just for traveling, this app acts as a torch and a magnifying glass all in one.

- **National Geographic Traveler**. Subscribe to this app to get an endless supply of high-quality travel features, photography and travel ideas.

- **New York Subway – MTA map and route planner**. Use this app to help you get around the Big Apple via the Subway. Plan your journeys and view live updates about stations and routes.

There are apps for displaying train times and details, but these are usually specific to your geographical location rather than covering a range of different countries.

- **P&O Cruises**. Find some of your favorite cruises with this app, which displays the full brochure of P&O Cruises.

- **Paris Travel Guide and Offline City Map**. A free map app for travel options around one of the great cities in the world.

- **Phrasebook**. Keep up with what the locals are saying in different countries with this app, which has useful phrases in 25 languages.

The Phrasebook app comes with one free language. After that, you have to pay a small fee for each language that you want to use.

...cont'd

- **Places You Must See in Your Lifetime**. A collection of stunning and unforgettable destinations and locations around the world. Impressive photography makes it all the more appealing, and you can also browse maps.

- **Sixt Rent a Car**. Use this app for car rental in 90 countries around the world.

- **Translator (Free)**. If you do not have the time or inclination to learn a new language, try this app to translate over 26 different languages.

- **Urbanspoon**. Another app for finding restaurants, with reviews, ratings and menus, in locations around the world (iPhone only; see tip on page 176). Covers the USA, Canada, UK, Australia and New Zealand.

- **Weather Live Free**. An app for showing the weather in locations around the world, with graphically-appealing forecasts, including extended forecasts for any coming day of the week or hour.

- **WiFi Finder**. It is always useful to be able to access Wi-Fi when you are on vacation, and sometimes essential. This app locates Wi-Fi hotspots in over two million locations worldwide.

- **Yelp**. Covering a range of information, this app locates restaurants, shops, services and places of interest in cities around the world.

12 Practical Matters

This chapter looks at security, locating a lost device, and financial matters using the iPad.

Setting Restrictions

Within the iPad Settings app, there are options for restricting types of content that can be viewed and actions that can be performed. These include:

- Turning off certain apps so they cannot be used

- Enabling changes to certain functions

- Restricting content that is viewed when using specific apps

After setting restrictions, they can be locked so that no-one else can change them. To set and lock restrictions:

Hot tip

It is a good idea to set up some restrictions on your iPad if young children or grandchildren are going to have access to it.

1 Tap once on the **Settings** app

2 Tap once on the **General** tab

3 Tap once on the **Restrictions** option

Restrictions	Off >

4 The Restrictions are grayed-out; i.e. they have not been enabled for use yet

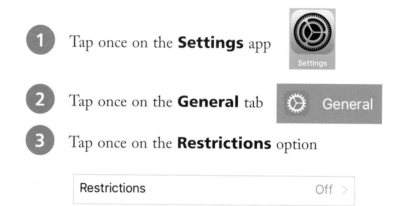

5 Tap once on the **Enable Restrictions** link

Enable Restrictions

6 Type on the keypad to set a passcode for enabling and disabling restrictions

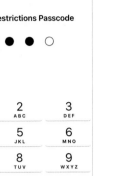

7 Re-enter the passcode

If you forget the passcode for unlocking your iPad it will become disabled after you have entered the wrong passcode six times. It can be reset by using a computer with which the iPad was last synced, and there are details about this on the Apple website Support pages (**https://support.apple.com**). However, to avoid this, ensure that you have a note of your iPad's passcode, but keep it away from the iPad.

8 All of the Restrictions options become available. Drag these buttons **On** or **Off** to disable certain apps. If an item is **Off** it will no longer be visible on the Home screen. Tap once on the options under **Allowed Content** to specify restrictions for certain types of content, such as music, movies, books and apps

You will need to turn apps back **On** in the Restrictions window in Step 8 to view hidden apps again.

Finding your iPad

No-one likes to think the worst, but if your iPad is lost or stolen, help is at hand. The Find My iPad function (operated through the iCloud service) allows you to send a message and an alert to a lost iPad, and also remotely lock it or even wipe its contents. This gives added peace of mind, knowing that even if your iPad is lost or stolen, its contents will not necessarily be compromised. To set up Find My iPad (before it becomes lost or stolen):

1. Tap once on the **Settings** app

2. Tap once on the **Apple ID** account option

3. Tap once on the **iCloud** button

4. Tap once on the **Find My iPad** option

5. Drag the **Find My iPad** button to **On** to be able to find your iPad on a map

Finding a lost iPad

Once you have set up Find My iPad you can search for it through the iCloud service, using another device. To do this:

1. Log in to your iCloud account at **www.icloud.com**

2. Click once on the **Find iPhone** button (this also works for the iPad)

Hot tip

Location Services must be turned **On** to enable the Find My iPad service (**Settings** > **Privacy** and turn **Location Services** On).

Hot tip

Another app that can be used to find a lost device is Lookout, which can be downloaded from the App Store.

...cont'd

3 Click once on the **All Devices** button and select your iPad. It is identified, and its current location is displayed on the map

4 Click once on the green circle to view details about when your iPad was located

Click once on the **Erase iPad** button in Step 5 to delete the iPad's contents. It is extremely important to have previously backed up your iPad content using iCloud (**Settings** > **Apple ID** > **iCloud** > **iCloud Backup** to **On**) so that you can restore the content to a new device, or your original one if it is found.

5 Click once here to send a sound alert to your iPad. This can be useful if you have lost it in the house or close by

6 Click once here to lock your iPad

7 Enter a message that will appear on the iPad. Its existing 6-digit passcode will then be required to unlock it (if it does not have one, you will be prompted to add one)

If you are using Family Sharing (see pages 64-68) you can use the Find Friends app to locate the devices of other Family Sharing members.

Avoiding Viruses

As far as security from viruses on the iPad is concerned, there is good news and bad news:

- The good news is that, due to its architecture, most apps on the iPad do not communicate with each other so, even if there were a virus, it is unlikely that it would infect the whole iPad. Also, there are relatively few viruses being aimed at the iPad, particularly compared to those for Windows PCs.

- The bad news is that no computer system is immune from viruses and malware, and complacency is one of the biggest enemies of computer security. There have been some instances of photos in iCloud being accessed and hacked, but this was more to do with password security, or lack of, rather than viruses.

iPad security

Apple takes security on the iPad very seriously, and one way that this manifests itself is in the fact it is designed so that different apps do not talk to each other. This means that if there were a virus in an app, it would be hard for it to transfer to other apps and therefore spread across the iPad. Apple checks apps very rigorously, but even this is not foolproof, as shown in various attacks that have taken place against Apple devices.

Antivirus options

There are a few apps in the App Store that deal with antivirus issues, but do not actually remove viruses:

- **McAfee**. The online security firm has a number of apps that cover issues such as privacy of data and password security.

- **Norton**. Another popular online security option that has a range of apps to check for viruses and malware.

- **F-Secure SAFE**. Although not an antivirus app, this can be used to check websites that you are browsing, to alert you to suspicious sites and keep your details secure.

Malware is short for malicious software, designed to harm your computer, or access and distribute information from it.

Apple also checks apps that are provided through the App Store, and this process is very robust. This does not mean that it is impossible for a virus to infect the iPad, so keep an eye on the Apple website to see if there are any details about iPad viruses.

Dealing with Money

We all like to keep track of our money and, although it may not be as much fun as reading books or looking at photos, it is a necessary task that can be undertaken on the iPad.

Some general financial apps are looked at on page 186, but one of the most common platforms for financial matters is online banking. This is where you can use banking apps from your account provider to access your bank accounts. (Online banking sites can also be accessed through the web using Safari.)

Banking apps are tailored to your geographical location, i.e. the banks that operate in your country. Most banking apps operate in a similar way:

Beware

If you are logging into your online banking service, make sure any "Remember Me" login details options are unchecked, particularly if other people have access to your iPad.

1 You have to first register for the online service. Once you have done this, tap on the **Log on** button to enter your account details

2 You can now access your bank accounts, view balances and transfer money. General information is also available through the app, such as branch locations and contact details

Don't forget

If you are looking to move home, there are a lot of real-estate apps that provide high-quality color photos of all parts of properties for sale. As with banking apps, real-estate apps are tailored to your geographical location and they all have a Search facility for looking for properties in different areas. The search results can usually be filtered by criteria such as price, number of bedrooms and property type.

Financial Apps

Within the Finance category of the App Store there are apps for managing your personal finances, viewing share prices and organizing your bank accounts and bills. Some to look at are:

- **Account Tracker**. A useful app for keeping track of your expenditure. It can be used to monitor multiple bank accounts and also set alerts and reminders for paying bills.

- **Bloomberg**. This is an app for following stocks and shares. You can add any shares that you own, and view live prices while markets are open (with a 15-minute delay). There is also a financial news service.

- **Calculator**. For working out your own finances, there are several calculators providing large, attractive interfaces with plenty of functionality.

- **HomeBudget**. An app for managing your household income and expenses. It also supports charts and graphs so you can compare expenditure over periods of time.

- **Meter Readings**. Useful for keeping an eye on your home fuel consumption, this app helps you to save money by monitoring your utility readings. Enter the readings, and your usage and costs are displayed in user-friendly graphs to show where savings can be made.

- **Money for iPad**. As well as being used to manage bills and view all of your accounts, this app also provides useful planning features and reminders.

- **Pocket Expense**. Another in the range of apps with which you can monitor bank accounts, track bills, view transactions and see where you can save money.

- **SharePrice**. Another app for seeing how your share portfolio is doing. Real-time share information, market news and profit/loss details are provided.

- **Spending Tracker**. Another general finance app for managing your money and monitoring budgets.

Hot tip

With your iPad and an internet connection, you should always be able to keep an eye on your shares portfolio, as well as buying and selling shares wherever you are.

Index

189